1999 FACTS ABOUT BLACKS

1999 FACTS ABOUT BLACKS

A Sourcebook of African-American Accomplishment

Raymond M. Corbin

Illustrations by Barbara Higgins Bond

Beckham House PUBLISHERS, INC

Published in the United States by
Beckham House Publishers, Inc.

ISBN: 0-931761-06-9, paper

10 9 8 7 6 5

First Edition

TABLE OF CONTENTS

The following Brown University undergraduates served as research assistants for this project: Joseph Amodio, Dorothy Bisbee, Joseph A. Hafner and Angela Mitchell.

I would like to dedicate this book to my mother, Mrs. Pearl Corbin; to a very dear friend, Mary Sutton for her patience; Loretta Sutton for typing, and a special friend, Richard White who stood by me all the way. I would also like to thank Barry Beckham who is not only the publisher but also has been a good friend for over thirty years. To all of you: thank you very much.

HISTORY

Above (l. to r.): Thurgood Marshall; A. Philip Randolph; Booker T. Washington; Harriet Tubman. *Below:* Richard Allen; John Russwurm.

HISTORY

1. The history of black America began when a ship carrying 20 blacks landed in what city?

2. This black cabinetmaker built a wooden automobile.

3. Who was the first man to pilot a plane across the United States?

4. Who published the first African-American periodical?

5. Who was the first African-American to head the country's largest municipal public welfare program in New York City?

6. He convened the first Pan-African Congress in Paris in 1919.

7. In what year did Marcus Garvey arrive in Harlem?

8. He was the first black Rhodes Scholar in 1907.

3

9. In what year did the first African-Americans arrive here?

10. According to John Winthrop's *Journal* the first African slaves were brought to New England in what year?

11. Name the ship on which the first black slaves arrived in New England.

12. In 1641, this colony became the first to recognize slavery as a legal institution.

13. What was the first item ever patented by an African-American inventor?

14. Which colony became the first to pass laws forbidding marriage between black men and white women in 1664?

15. The first formal anti-slavery resolution was adopted by what religious group in 1688?

16. His New York City school, established in 1704, was one of the first for African-Americans.

17. He is considered the first to die in the Boston Massacre of 1770.

18. He bought his freedom with profits from the sale of smoking tobacco.

19. He was the first wholesaler, first merchant prince, and the first settler in Chicago.

20. Who, in 1834, was the first African-American to receive a U.S. patent?

21. Which state became the first to abolish slavery in 1777?

22. On November 12, 1775, this general issued an order

that forbade black enlistment in the army.

23. Male slaves who joined the British army during the Revolution were promised this.

24. A section that denounced slavery was deleted from this document before its adoption in 1776.

25. The first African-American church was established in 1773 in this Southern city.

26. What black worker designed a railroad car coupling device for which a New York railroad paid $50,000 in 1897?

27. In 1900 Booker T. Washington formed this business organization in Boston.

28. Who founded the North Carolina Mutual Life Insurance Company?

29. The first Abolitionist Society was established in this city in 1775.

30. The Continental Congress prohibited slavery in this part of the country in 1787.

31. He was a member of the commission that surveyed the District of Columbia in 1791.

32. When was the slave trade banned by Congress?

33. Name the first bank operated for blacks.

34. The American Insurance Company of Philadelphia, the first managed by blacks, was established in what year?

35. Who led the slave conspiracy involving thousands of blacks in Charleston, S.C. and surrounding areas?

36. Considered the first black to receive a degree from an

American college, he graduated from Middlebury College in 1823.

37. What was the name of the first black newspaper, published in 1827?

38. He was the first black Roman Catholic bishop in America.

39. This black associate of Thomas Alva Edison drafted plans for the first electric street light.

40. This businessman founded the town of Mound Bayou, Mississippi.

41. In what year did the first national black convention meet?

42. He issued his first almanac in 1792.

43. By what name was black inventor Andrew J. Beard's railroad car coupling device popularly known?

44. Who was elected president of the first national black convention held in Philadelphia?

45. Who led the slave rebellion in Southampton County, Virginia on August 21-23, 1831, in which 60 whites were killed?

46. How many African-American newspapers were published before the civil war?

47. What was the name of the first anti-slavery political party, organized in 1839?

48. Between 1872 and 1920 he received over 57 patents for automatic lubricating appliances.

49. H. C. Haynes of Chicago invented this item.

50. Who was the first black to serve a full term in the United States Senate?

51. He was the first black lawyer admitted to the bar in 1945.

52. How many autobiographies did Frederick Douglass write?

53. She escaped from slavery in 1849 and made 19 trips back to the South to rescue more than 300 slaves.

54. Inventions for automatically lubricating railroad cars were not considered authentic unless stamped with what slang expression denoting authenticity?

55. What magazine publishes the only listing of America's most successful black-owned companies?

56. In 1913 he started the Standard Life Insurance Company of Atlanta.

57. Who published *Services of Colored Americans in the Wars of 1776 and 1812*, the first extended history of black Americans?

58. He published *The Constitution, Elevation, Emigration, and Destiny of the Colored People of the United States*, the first major statement of the black nationalist position.

59. What act of Congress opened the Northern territory to slavery in 1854?

60. What 1857 U.S. Supreme Court decision denied that blacks were citizens?

61. Shelby J. Davidson invented this office device.

62. Who sold his patented shoe soling machine to the

United Shoe Machinery Company of Boston in 1883?   ✓

63. In 1982 this black-owned company was the largest independent data processing and computer security firm in the country.

64. What lieutenant governor of Louisiana was born a slave in 1826 in New Orleans, and operated an employment service for former slaves?

65. What act of Congress protected the slaves against all rebels in 1862?

66. Contrary to popular belief, this measure did *not* free all ✓ slaves.

67. What was the name of the newspaper published by ✓ Frederick Douglass?

68. He was the first black to win the Congressional Medal of Honor for the attack on Fort Wagner in Charleston, S.C. ✓ in 1863.

69. What was the name of the first black daily newspaper?

70. In what year did Congress pass the 13th Amendment ✓ to the Constitution, abolishing slavery in America?

71. What was the largest black bank in 1981, with assets of $101.9 million?

72. His bakery employed a large number of freedmen during the Civil War.

73. Who was the first African-American awarded a Ph.D. ✓ degree?

74. These laws enacted by some Southern states restricted movement of free blacks.

75. In what year was the first Civil Rights Act passed?

76. On March 2, 1866, this became the first Southern city to allow blacks to vote.

77. This organization, known for terrorizing blacks, held its first national meeting in Nashville in April, 1887.

78. Who invented the gas mask and the first electric stoplight signal?

79. In what year was the Independence Bank of Chicago founded?

80. This Virgin Islander played a major role in the political struggle over the possession of California between the U. S. and Mexico.

81. Who became the first black cabinet officer at the state level when he was installed as the secretary of the state of South Carolina?

82. When installed as lieutenant governor of Louisiana in 1868, he became the highest ranked black elected official.

83. He became the first black to hold a major judicial position when he was elected to the South Carolina Supreme Court in 1870.

84. He was the first black U.S. Senator.

85. This New Orleans machinist and engineer was responsible for inventing a patented multi-effect vacuum evaporating process which revolutionized sugar refining methods in 1945.

86. She was the first African-American woman lawyer in 1872.

87. He was the first black student at the U.S. Naval

Academy in 1872.

88. He became the first African-American to head a predominantly white university when he was inaugurated as president of Georgetown University in 1874. ✓

89. The first black to receive a Ph.D. degree from an American university received his degree in physics from what school?

90. He was the first black graduate from West Point. ✓

91. In what year was the largest black insurance firm founded?

92. What college was established by Booker T. Washington in 1881?

93. This state began the modern segregation movement in 1881 with the introduction of the Jim Crow railroad car.

94. In 1884, he became the first black to chair a national political party when he was elected temporary chairman of the Republican Party.

95. The first African-American bank, Capital Savings Bank, opened here in 1888.

96. Name the first training school for black nurses located in Chicago.

97. This scientist developed early rockets for the United States government. ✓

98. This Fulbright Fellow was also alternate executive director of the U. S. World Bank.

99. What black physician performed the first successful heart operation at Chicago's Provident Hospital in 1893? ✓

100. What is the name of the black medical association founded in Atlanta in 1895?

101. What Supreme Court decision upheld the "separate but equal" doctrine and began the age of Jim Crow in 1896?

102. She became the first black woman to head a bank when named president of St. Luke Bank and Trust Company in 1903 in Richmond, Va.

103. He was the first black member of the Federal Parole Board.

104. On one occasion, the city of New Orleans borrowed money from this wealthy African-American.

105. What civil rights organization was founded by 47 whites and six blacks in 1907?

106. Who was the first editor of *The Crisis*, the periodical of the NAACP?

107. Which city was the first to enact ordinances requiring white and black residential areas?

108. Which president segregated blacks and whites in government departments in 1913?

109. What bacteriologist developed the test for syphilis?

110. What Baltimore paper was founded by John Henry Murphy?

111. Who developed devices for registering calls and detecting unauthorized telephone use?

112. When did the great migration of blacks from the South to Northern cities begin?

113. What did Madame C.J. Walker manufacture?

114. How many riots occurred during the "Red Summer" of 1919?

115. What was the first black periodical?

116. When was Phi Beta Sigma Fraternity founded?

117. In what year were the first Doctor of Philosophy degrees awarded to African-American women?

118. In what year was Zeta Phi Beta Sorority founded?

119. Who organized the first Negro History Week? ∨

120. What association of black lawyers was incorporated in 1926?

121. What was the percentage of black males unemployed in 1937, at the height of the Great Depression?

122. He was the first black Democratic congressman.

123. In what year did the U.S. Supreme Court rule that ✓ states must provide equal education facilities for blacks?

124. She became the first black woman judge in 1939.

125. What famous black chemist obtained more than 100 ✓ patents?

126. He was the second president of the North Carolina Mutual Insurance Company.

127. What type of company was the oldest black business according to a list compiled by *Black Enterprise* in 1980?

128. What is the largest black insurance company, with $190 million in assets and 1,400 employees?

129. This black businessman and politician died in 1848 leaving a $1.5 million estate, the bulk of which came from his land on the American River, one site of the 1849 gold rush.

130. Who was the first African-American general in the United States?

131. She became the first black woman lawmaker when elected to the Pennsylvania legislature in 1938.

132. What does CORE stand for?

133. He invented the incandescent electric light bulb in collaboration with the noted inventor, Hiram S. Maxim.

134. Who founded the North Carolina Mutual Life Insurance Company?

135. In what year was the first issue of *Ebony* magazine published?

136. Who was the first black graduate of the U.S. Naval Academy?

137. Which president ordered "equality of treatment and opportunity in the armed forces"?

138. In what city was WERD, the first black-owned radio station, opened in 1949?

139. She was the first black representative in the U.S. delegation to the United Nations.

140. Which African-American was touted as the "greatest electrician in the world" by the American *Catholic Tribune* in 1888?

141. This civil rights leader was co-editor and co-publisher of the *Boston Guardian*.

142. He was the first black awarded the Nobel Peace Prize, in 1950.

143. In what Illinois city did a mob of 3,500 keep a black family from moving?

144. Tuskegee Institute reported that this was the first year in 71 years that there were no lynchings in America.

145. How long did the Trumbull Park housing project riots last in Chicago?

146. This scientist holds more than 75 patents related to meat packing and food preservation.

147. Robert L. Vann founded and published this Pittsburgh periodical.

148. What landmark Supreme Court decision declared segregation in public schools unconstitutional in 1954?

149. Who was the first black general in the U.S. Air Force?

150. She is famous for not moving to the back of the bus in Montgomery, Alabama in 1955.

151. Who was the first president of the Southern Christian Leadership Conference?

152. He was the first African-American to head a major national veterans organization.

153. Who was called "the Black Edison"?

154. Who was the founder and president of the Universal Life Insurance Company?

155. He founded Barfield Industries of Ypsilanti, Michigan in 1955.

156. Which city was the first to pass laws against racial or religious discrimination in housing in 1957?

157. For what does SNCC stand?

158. This leader of the Nation of Islam called for the creation of a black state in America in 1960.

159. In 1885, he obtained Patent No. 315,368 for the "telegraphony," a device that receives and transmits Morse code or voice messages.

160. He was allowed to register at the University of Mississippi after government intervention in 1962.

161. Four black girls were killed when this Birmingham church was bombed in 1963.

162. This NAACP field secretary was assassinated in front of his home in Jackson, Mississippi in 1963.

163. Who founded the Organization for Afro-American Unity in 1964?

164. He received a Nobel Peace Prize in 1964, becoming the third black and the youngest person ever to receive the award.

165. Who compiled a four-volume source of inventions by African-Americans while serving as assistant examiner in the U.S. Patent Office?

166. This lawyer founded the National Negro Publishers Association.

167. What black inventor's shoe soling machine was known as "The Lasting Machine"?

168. Who introduced horseracing to California on his

35,000 acre tract of land on the American River?

169. The Hinton Test aids in the diagnosis of this communicable disease.

170. What was the first magazine to be edited by an African-American?

171. He was assassinated in the Audubon Ballroom in 1965.

172. She became the first African-American woman ambassador when appointed to Luxembourg in 1965.

173. J.W. Benton made the walk from his home in Kentucky to the Patent Office in Washington D.C., carrying a model of this invention.

174. He launched the Black Power movement in 1966.

175. Who was the first black woman federal judge?

176. He patented a device for handling sails and later owned a sailmaking factory in Philadelphia.

177. This group represented the first efforts to organize blacks in business.

178. Huey Newton and this gentleman founded the Black Panther Party in 1966.

179. How many U.S. cities reported racial violence in 1966?

180. He was the first black sheriff in the South in the 20th century.

181. In 1967, the U. S. Supreme Court ruled that a law banning interracial marriage in this state was unconstitutional.

182. He became the first black Supreme Court justice in ✓ 1967.

183. This free black inventor became one of the richest men in Philadelphia and helped finance William Lloyd Garrison's *Liberator*.

184. In 1865, the leading business of this type in Boston was conducted by a black man.

185. In what year was the First National Black Economic Summit convened?

186. Who was the first black astronaut? ✓

187. He became the first black mayor of a major American ✓ city in 1967.

188. She was the first woman in the history of Howard University to receive a B. S. degree in chemical engineering.

189. In 1968, she founded National Domestics, a pioneer group that attempted to organize household workers.

190. She founded the Veterans Administration Independent Service Employees Credit Union in the early 1970's.

191. Who was the first black member of the New York Stock Exchange?

192. She is the founder and president of Trade Union Women of African Heritage.

193. Who was the first black woman to chair the NAACP?

194. Students at this university seized the administration building and demanded a black-oriented curriculum in 1968.

195. Who was the first African-American nominated for

president by a major national party in 1968?

196. Who was the first black woman elected to Congress?

197. In 1930, at the age of 24, this African-American inventor was teaching applied mathematics at l'Ecole Centrale in Paris.

198. Who is recognized by *Ebony* magazine as "the first Negro capitalist"?

199. What Democratic Representative from Maryland convened the First National Black Economic Summit in Baltimore?

200. Fred Hampton and this Black Panther leader were killed in a Chicago police raid in 1969.

201. For what do the initials PUSH, the acronym for Rev. Jesse Jackson's organization, stand?

202. He became the first black Secretary of the Army in 1977.

203. In 1881, he developed the standard system for refining sugar, as well as glue, gelatin and condensed milk.

204. He resigned as UN Ambassador after an unauthorized meeting with representatives of the Palestinian Liberation Organization in 1979.

205. Who was the first African-American to head an embassy in Europe?

206. He became in 1920 the first black executive secretary of the NAACP.

207. He was the first black to head a major agency of the U.S. government, as administrator of the Housing and Home Finance Agency.

208. Who became the first black diplomat to receive a major government appointment when named minister to Haiti in 1869?

209. A national boycott by People United to Save Humanity in 1981 forced this company to put $34 million into black businesses.

210. He was the only black member of the "Edison Pioneers," a privileged group working with Thomas Edison.

211. Prior to 1900, he operated one of Boston's largest clothing stores.

212. He was the first black governor of the Federal Reserve Board in 1966.

213. In what year was SNCC organized?

214. Who was the first African-American to co-chair a national political convention?

215. She was the first African-American keynote speaker of a national political convention.

216. He became the first black governor when governor Warmoth of Louisiana was impeached in 1872.

217. What invention did James Smith, J.L. Pickering, W.G. Madison and H.E. Hooker all patent?

218. John Jones of Chicago made a million dollars at this occupation.

219. He co-founded the Black Ford Lincoln-Mercury Dealers Association.

220. He became the first black physician in 1783.

221. He was the first black to graduate from an American medical college.

222. Who was the first African-American admitted to a medical society in 1854?

223. He was the first black inducted in Phi Beta Kappa in 1874.

224. This leader of the Tuskegee Methodist Church initiated the founding of Tuskegee Institute.

225. While at the U. S. Bureau of Standards, he invented a device used to test the durability of leather.

226. He became the first black to get his Ph.D. from Harvard for a dissertation on the African slave trade in the U.S.

227. In what year was the United Negro College Fund established?

228. This black mathematician and astronomer published 10 almanacs between 1792 and 1802.

229. What famous black asserted, "The history of the world is the history not of individuals, but of groups, not of nations but of races..."?

230. Many Northern whites supported the education of blacks in the eighteenth century so that they could read this book.

231. The end of this historical event helped spark the Harlem Renaissance.

232. Which black writer did Winston Churchhill quote with the words, "If we must die -- let it be not like hogs..." in his famous World War II speech?

233. Alice Dunnigan, the first black woman correspondent for the White House, covered the campaign of what president?

234. By what percentage did the black population in major U.S. cities rise between 1921 and 1923?

235. What black served as advisor to President Lincoln, and as Consul General to the Republic of Haiti under President Harrison?

236. In 1970, this state's legislature ruled that any person with 1/32 "black blood" was African-American.

237. She joined the civil rights movement during the bus boycott of 1955, and became alderwoman of Chicago's Third Ward in 1984.

238. Who was elected mayor of Oakland, CA in 1977?

239. A black marrying a white in the nineteenth century in the U.S. could be imprisoned for up to how many years?

240. How many states counted more than 20% blacks in their 1980 Census?

241. His work ethic caused black schools in the rural South to reject art education as frivolous.

242. Best known for her autobiography, this ex-slave taught at Wilberforce Academy and founded the Contraband Relief Association in 1862.

243. In Philadelphia, where they were legal, how many interracial marriages were counted in 1900?

244. The son of a black man and a white woman, he served as a consultant on theology to the presidents of Yale and Amherst, and is famous for his 1795 sermon, *Universal Salvation*.

245. William Stanley Braithwaite joined the English faculty of this first graduate school for African-Americans in 1930.

246. The oldest African-American periodical, it celebrated its centennial in 1984.

247. Who was the first black elected to the Mississippi legislature, in 1967?

248. This lawyer from Jacksonville, Florida was elected president of the National Business League in 1984.

249. Who became chief judge of the Washington, D.C. Court of Appeals in 1984?

250. In 1984, African-Americans held what government post in Newark, Detroit, Atlanta, Philadelphia and Chicago?

251. Who became Washington editor of *Ebony* and *Jet* magazines in 1984?

252. In Jackson, Mississippi, this dental surgeon, businessman and former head of the NAACP was the first African-American to have a federal building named after him.

253. The Birmingham, Alabama Rotary Club admitted its first African-American member in what year?

254. What post did Samuel Pierce hold in 1984, when he was the highest-ranked minority member of President Reagan's cabinet?

255. During the Carter Administration, she became the first black woman HUD secretary.

256. The first black congresswoman in Indiana, she was nicknamed "the hoosier lady."

257. Dr. Will Herzfeld was the first African-American to be elected bishop of what church in 1984?

258. What president appointed Andrew Young ambassador to the United Nations?

259. What had former Brooklyn, N. Y. street gang leader Robert "Sonny" Carson changed his name to by the time he became head of the Congress of Racial Equality?

260. Julia Clarice Brown, who had earlier joined the Communist Party and been active in the civil rights movement, worked for this organization from 1951 to 1960.

261. How many states were still banning interracial marriage in 1969?

262. What organization did the author of *Sand Against the Wind: The Memoirs of John C. Dancy* head for 42 years?

263. He became mayor of Ypsilanti, Michigan after 18 years on the city council.

264. George D. Carroll became mayor of this city in 1964.

265. How many years did Malcolm X spend in jail?

266. Who was the first black to earn his first mate's license, in 1918, and the first black captain of a U.S. Merchant Marine ship, in 1942?

267. Having attended Colgate and Columbia Universities and served as a Baptist minister in Harlem, he started his tenure in the U.S. House of Representatives in 1944.

268. The author of *Notes of a Processed Brother*, he helped establish a bill of rights in 1969-1970 for New York City public high school students.

269. *Black Man in Red Russia: A Memoir* relates his

experiences as a foreign correspondent in the U.S.S.R. from 1932 to 1946.

270. A scientist and brother of Howard University President Emeritus James Nabrit, he became the first black to receive a Ph.D. from Brown University in 1932.

271. In addition to owning and editing the *California Eagle*, a Los Angeles newspaper, she was the U.S. vice-presidential candidate for the Progressive Party in 1948.

272. What U.S. congresswoman attempted to win the Democratic Party presidential nomination in 1972?

273. Eldridge Cleaver is best known for his involvement in what organization?

274. What was Malcolm X's original name?

275. Who became the mayor of Chapel Hill, North Carolina in 1968?

276. What city did James H. McGee become mayor of in 1969?

277. Who was Administrator for Special Projects in the White House from 1955 to 1961?

278. She relates her experiences as a Vietnam war correspondent in 1966-1967 in her book, *Good Men Die*.

279. How many black newspapers were there in the U.S. in 1975?

280. After he had signed the Voting Rights Act of 1965, the number of black voters in the South nearly tripled.

281. Who wrote *Dark Ghetto: Dilemmas of Social Power*.

282. What percent of the population was black in 1800?

283. What U.S. city, along with Washington, D.C., Atlanta, Georgia, and Newark, New Jersey, had a black majority in 1975?

284. In a controversial 1965 report called *The Negro Family: The Case for National Action,* this white writer asserted that black families were becoming increasingly unstable.

285. What African-American became mayor of Richmond, California in 1971?

286. Theodore Berry was elected mayor of this city in 1972.

287. What percentage of Southern black children attended desegregated schools in 1960?

288. Who on March 21, 1974 asked for anti-busing legislation?

289. In 1965, it became the first state to pass a racial imbalance law, which defined schools having 50% nonwhites as racially imbalanced.

290. METCO (the Metropolitan Council for Educational Opportunities) and Operation Exodus accomplished limited busing to the suburbs of what city?

291. What was the best known New York City street academy, or alternate school for black high school dropouts, in the 'seventies?

292. Located in Ohio, it was one of the first two U.S. black universities founded in the mid-1800's.

293. In the landmark Supreme Court decision of 1938, what school was ordered to admit Lloyd Gaines?

294. Between 1964 and 1968, less than what percentage of Ph.D.s were awarded to blacks?

295. Which U.S. president's Executive Order 11063 prohibited discrimination in the administration of federally funded housing?

296. What was the first organization to have the formation of a separate nation for blacks in the U.S. as its goal?

297. The first black mayor of Atlantic City, New Jersey, he is a former superintendent of schools.

298. What black congressman successfully fought for the commemoration of African-American women in a series of postage stamps?

299. This Boston agency was founded in 1963 to help gifted minority high school students to obtain quality educations.

300. Issued by the African Methodist Episcopal Church, it is the oldest black church periodical existing today.

301. What black sorority, established at Howard University in 1908, has chapters in 46 states and publishes *Ivy Leaf Magazine?*

302. Founded at Cornell in 1906, it is the oldest black fraternity in the nation.

303. When was the all-black American Bridge Association founded?

304. This fraternal order consists of Nobles and Daughters of Isis, and focuses its charitable efforts on combatting drug abuse and diseases that strike blacks.

305. Chi Eta Phi Sorority is an organization made up of American and West-African black women professionals in what field?

306. The first African-American to join a masonic order, he established his own order that counts a membership of over 250,000 today.

307. Consisting of the blacks in the U.S. House of Representatives, this organization was founded in 1970.

308. At what college was Delta Sigma Theta Sorority, Inc., founded in 1913?

309. Established in 1898, this African-American order publishes *Elk News*, a quarterly newsletter.

310. This black fraternity, now numbering over 80,000 members, was founded at Indiana University in 1911.

311. What must members of the Most Worshipful National Grand Lodge believe in?

312. What major U.S. organization runs the ACT-SO Program (Afro-Academic, Cultural, Technological and Scientific Olympics) which awards scholarships to blacks?

313. As of 1984, how many ski clubs belonged to the all-black National Brotherhood of Skiers?

314. In what New York City museum does the National Coalition of 100 Black Women hold its annual awards ceremony?

315. What organization publishes *The State of Black America* each year?

316. This black fraternity which counts over 80,000 members, was founded in 1911 at Howard University.

317. Talmadge Hayer, Norman 3X Butler and Thomas 15X Johnson, who were sentenced to life imprisonment on March 10, 1966 for first degree murder, belonged to what group?

318. In 1965, Vivian Malone was the first black to graduate from this institution.

319. In New Orleans in 1965 he became the first African-American to be appointed bishop.

320. Which European nation was the first to stop trading African slaves to America in 1794?

321. In what year was the Ku Klux Klan, Inc., founded?

322. The former director of the Southern Christian Leadership Conference, he was appointed special assistant on Urban Affairs to Governor Nelson Rockefeller.

323. The rate of unemployment in this part of Chicago was 35% in 1966.

324. He is the author of *The Negro Revolt,* which won second prize for reportage at the first World Festival of Negro Arts in Dakar, Senegal in 1966.

325. A prominent member of the Communist party who was convicted of plotting the overthrow of the U.S. government in 1953, he died in Moscow in 1965.

326. What black laborer discovered the body of Charles A. Lindbergh's kidnapped son in 1932?

327. A *Pitsburgh Courier* for over 40 years, he was the first African-American international news correspondent.

328. Who is considered the first black to have graduated from Bowdoin college in 1826?

329. He was 65 when he became the first black injured in the Civil War.

330. Who became the first black police officer to command

a Harlem district in 1963?

331. Who was the first African-American to win the title "Catholic Mother of the Year" in 1952?

332. Who was the first black woman principal of a New York City public school?

333. What New York paper did Timothy Thomas Fortune found in 1883?

334. He started four black magazines: *Negro Digest, Ebony, Tan,* and *Jet.*

335. A lawyer, she was the first African-American woman Ph.D.

336. An editor of the Memphis *Free Speech,* she crusaded against lynching in the South around the turn of the century.

337. He was elected mayor of Newark, NJ in 1970. ✓

338. Her 1962 book, *The Long Shadow of Little Rock,* tells of her efforts in the struggle to integrate schools in the South.

339. While serving a five-year prison term for subversion, he published *Communist Councilman from Harlem: Autobiographical Notes Written in a Federal Penitentiary* in 1969.

340. Between 1905 and 1912 this teacher, elocutionist and writer headed both the Ohio State Federation of Women and the National Association of Colored Women.

341. Previously an associate director of the Philadelphia *Christian Banner,* she founded the National Training School for Women and Girls in 1909.

342. What distinguished educational administrator earned a Ph.D. from the Sorbonne in 1922, at the age of 66, and lived to be 105 years old?

343. Dr. Dorothy B. Ferebee succeeded Mary McLeod Bethune as president of this organization.

344. Who became the first black woman to be appointed by the President to a U.S. judgeship, in 1962?

345. In his 1971 book, *When God Was Black,* he relates his experiences as a participant in Billy Graham's religious crusades.

346. Author of *The Negro Woman's College Education,* she was named "one of the 100 most influential Negroes of the Emancipation Centennial Year" by *Ebony* magazine in 1963.

347. Who became Director of the Women's Job Corps in 1965?

348. The U.S. Supreme Court ordered the desegregation of what state's prisons in 1968?

349. In what year did Yale University decide to offer a B.A. in Afro-American studies?

350. A 1969 strike of Charlestown, North Carolina hospital workers evolved into a major civil rights movement that lasted 113 days and was led by this organization.

351. His book, *Life and Works of a Negro Detective,* chronicles his experiences in Dayton, Ohio, near the turn of the century.

352. Marine Sgt. Rodney M. Davis was the tenth black man to receive the Medal of Honor for service in Vietnam; how many blacks in military history had received the Medal of Honor previously?

353. In 1969, following an overnight occupation of the student union at this university, about 100 black students emerged with shotguns and rifles.

354. Who succeeded Dr. Martin Luther King, Jr. as head of the Southern Christian Leadership Conference?

355. The Department of Health, Education and Welfare ruled in 1969 that this college could exclude whites from black studies classes on the grounds that their backgrounds were not relevant.

356. What Howard University president served as an Ambassador to the U.S. delegation to the United Nations in 1965?

357. An executive with the United Church of Christ, he was one of the "Wilmington Ten," civil rights activists sentenced to 282 years in prison in 1972.

358. Who was the first black to become a professor at Harvard Medical School, in 1949?

359. A U. S. District Judge, he became Yale University's first African-American trustee in 1970.

360. In 1970, he became the first Southern black minister in the history of the United Methodist Church to lead an all-white congregation.

361. In Washington, D.C. in 1970, he became the first black superintendent of schools in a major American city.

362. What company was the first major multinational to elect a black to its board of directors, naming Dr. Leon Howard Sullivan in 1971?

363. Who ordered the desegregation of Boston schools in 1974?

364. What is the formal name of the Black Muslims?

365. A navy destroyer escort has been named after this man, who was the first African-American aviator and the first black naval officer to be killed in the Korean War.

366. In what city was the major black newspaper, *Afro-American,* founded in 1892?

367. What philanthropic organization awarded $100 million to black colleges during the 'seventies?

368. In 1972, Kerry Pourcain became the first black president of this university.

369. An attorney and Baptist minister, he was the first African-American to serve on the Federal Communications Commission.

370. This comedian, civil rights leader, former track star and essayist published *Nigger: An Autobiography* in 1964.

371. Who became the first black director of the American Library Association in 1972?

372. Assigned to Europe in 1972, this Major General was the first black to command a U.S. Army division.

373. An all-white jury convicted her of murder, kidnapping and conspiracy for a 1970 shootout that killed four people.

374. Who is the black security guard that caught five men breaking into the Democratic National Headquarters in the Watergate complex?

375. Whose 1972 promotion to Major General made him the highest ranking black officer in the U.S. Air Force?

376. In 1972, the department of Housing and Urban

Development guaranteed $14 million in land development bonds to this new town in North Carolina; it was the first such program sponsored by an African-American.

377. What percentage of murder victims in the United States were black men in 1970?

378. Black servicemen Charles C. Rogers, Fred C. Sheffy and Roscoe Robinson were all promoted to what rank in 1973?

379. In what year did the Order of the Elks decide to admit blacks?

380. Started in 1973, it was the first black-owned and operated radio news network.

381. In 1974 he became the first African-American moderator of the Presbyterian Church.

382. In 1974, a federal judge ruled that unless the cultural bias was removed from these tests, black children in California should not register for them.

383. What civil rights activist was also the research chemist who isolated soya protein and held over 130 chemical patents?

384. According to the Council on Municipal Performance, what was the most racially segregated Northern city in 1975?

385. What black historian was chosen to give the fifth annual lecture for the National Council on Humanities in 1975?

386. The first private black medical college in the U.S., it celebrated its 100th anniversary in 1976.

387. Who was the first black president of the

predominantly white United Church of Christ in 1976?

388. In what year was the National Association of Black Journalists organized?

389. Dr. Henry A. Hill became the first black president of this organization in 1976.

390. In what city are the black periodicals *Black Stars, Daily Defender, Ebony, Jet,* and *Courier* published?

391. Who was tried in North Carolina for murder in 1975 because she had allegedly killed a white policeman in her struggle to stop him from raping her.

392. In 1958, an article in the *Ohio Journal of Science* estimated that one out of how many Americans had black ancestors?

393. During the nineteenth century, how many states had laws prohibiting interracial marriage?

394. For whom were the Manassah Society in Chicago and the Penguin Club in New York, founded in 1890 and 1936 respectively, organized?

395. Who founded Tuskegee Institute in 1881?

396. What is the name of the slave who was the first to explore much of Arizona and New Mexico?

397. A trader who once was chief of the Crow Indians, he discovered Pueblo, Colorado as well as a Sierra Nevada pass in California which is named for him.

398. A plaque in Annapolis, Maryland honors this black who took part in Admiral Perry's expedition to the North Pole.

399. This organization, which later became the American

Methodist Episcopal Church, was founded by Richard Allen and Absalom Jones in Philadelphia in 1877.

400. Located in Wisconsin and the oldest cement building in the U.S., this museum used to be a station on the Underground Railway.

401. An army interpreter who had lived with the Sioux, he is reputed to have been sitting beside Sitting Bull when he died.

402. A publisher of the *Atlanta Daily World*, he won the Georgia State Chamber of Commerce Citizens Award in 1959.

403. He became president and general manager of the Robert S. Abbott Publishing Co., which publishes the Chicago *Defender* and the *Tri-State Defender*, in 1940.

404. The first black leader of a racially mixed town in the South since Reconstruction, James Charles Evers was elected mayor of Fayette, Mississippi in what year?

405. In Gary, Indiana in 1967, he became the first African-American mayor of a major Northern city.

406. Elected mayor of Atlanta, Georgia in 1973, he became the first black mayor of a major Southeastern city.

407. The youngest of 20 in a sharecropping family, she founded the Mississippi Freedom Democratic Party.

408. Thomas Bradley became this city's first black elected official in 1963, and its first black mayor in 1973.

409. He served 21 years in the House of Representatives and five as chairman of the House Committee on Education and Labor.

410. He was considered the "recognized colored Republican leader" of New York City in the early twentieth century.

411. This church is the oldest African-American church in the North and was the largest Protestant church in America as well as a significant force in Harlem's history.

412. This Puerto Rican of African descent built one of the most important libraries devoted to African-Americans.

413. Established in 1972, it is the oldest black newspaper chain in the U.S.

414. What NAACP monthly did W.E.B. DuBois edit from 1911-1933?

415. What was the name of the newspaper edited by Frederick Douglass?

416. This politician became the first African-American to be elected to the City Council of New York.

417. The first black Rhodes Scholar and a professor of philosophy at Howard University, he published *The New Negro* in 1925.

418. What writer from Jamaica was associate editor of Max Eastman's *The Liberator*, and edited *The Masses* as well?

419. What black writer, who co-authored and co-starred with Ruby Dee in the movie *Up Tight,* started *The African Review* in 1962?

420. What black editor and literary critic published *Journal to Africa* in 1971?

421. Hoyt Fuller revitalized the literary magazine *Negro Digest* and changed its name to what in 1970?

422. Liberated from slavery by Union soldiers in 1865, this poet from North Carolina published in the *Liberator,* the *North Star,* and the Pennsylvania *Gazette.*

423. In what year was the Capital Press Club, the oldest African-American press organization, founded?

424. How many black commodity brokers operated on the New Orleans Cotton Exchange in the 1840s?

425. Who was the first black real estate broker?

426. What was the first black college, established in 1837?

427. Having become the first black to command a U. S. Navy ship in 1966, he was appointed the first black admiral in the U.S. Navy in 1971.

428. She became the first black woman to graduate from an American college when she received her degree from Oberlin College in 1862.

429. In 1929, who was the only black candy manufacturer in America?

430. She was the first black American woman to receive a dental degree from the University of Michigan in 1887.

431. Who founded Frontiers of America?

432. In what city did the first African-American real estate broker operate in 1849?

433. In what year did a black first start selling new cars?

434. The first black to attend the University of North Carolina Law School, he was national chairman of CORE in 1963.

435. Who was the first black woman general, appointed on Sept. 1, 1979?

436. What was the first major daily newspaper to be published by African-Americans in the twentieth century?

437. He was the first black elected to the board of the New York Stock Exchange in 1972.

438. In 1966, she became the first black woman admitted to the Mississippi bar.

439. He has four patents on various rockets, and has received acclaim from NASA and the President's Office of Science and Technology.

440. He invented a guided missle device and the artificial heart stimulator control unit.

441. She was the first black woman to be elected president of the Girl Scouts of America in 1975.

442. He established the Overton Hygienic Co., the Douglass National Bank and the Victory Life Insurance company.

443. Who was the first president of the Freedmen's Bank?

444. In 1893, he organized the Southern Aid and Insurance Company.

445. In 1891, she criticized the inadequate schooling of black children and was fired from her job as a school teacher.

446. What U. S. Army Sergeant developed an airframe center support, making greater rocket payloads possible by reducing deadweight?

447. She was the first African-American to attempt to desegregate the University of Alabama.

448. John Cornelius Asbury, a business man and civic

leader, was a member of this state's legislature.

449. In what year did Connie Slaughter, the first black alumna of the University of Mississippi, graduate?

450. Who was the first black president of NOW (the National Organization for Women)?

451. He specialized in heating and ventilating system engineering, and patented numerous related inventions.

452. She sat in the Chair of the Organization of Afro-American Unity in 1965 after the death of her brother, Malcolm X.

453. The wife of a Black Panther leader, she started *Babylon,* a black newspaper, in 1971.

454. Who became the first woman Black Panther Party head in 1975?

455. He invented the car record player "autophonic."

456. She founded the Harlem Consumer Education Council, a consumer-advocacy group, in 1961.

457. In 1976, Jewell Plumber Cobb became the first black woman dean of what women's college?

458. In 1898, he started the National Benefit Life Insurance Company.

459. What was the original name of the North Carolina Mutual Life Insurance Company?

460. What was the first black organization with a business orientation?

461. In 1823 this prominent Philadelphia sail maker was worth $100,000.

462. Who was the first African-American to practice as an accountant?

463. Who led a revolt of 1,000 slaves in Richmond, Virginia in 1800?

464. William Lloyd Garrison started this abolitionist newspaper in Boston in 1831.

465. Who was the first African-American state bank commissioner of Rhode Island?

466. In 1899, this dentist patented the first modern golf tee.

467. Who organized the Universal Negro Improvement Association?

468. He was known as "Father Divine" when he preached of a "heaven on earth" for blacks in the 1920's and '30's.

469. One of America's first African-American music teachers, he opened a music school in Newport, Massachusetts in 1791.

470. What was the first all-black religious denomination in the United States?

471. The American Colonization Society tried to ease racial problems by sending free blacks to this nation.

472. Of what magazine was Lerone Bennett, Jr. senior editor?

473. The wooden clock he constructed was probably the first to be built in the United States.

474. Percy Julian synthesized the drug physostigmine which is crucial to the treatment of what eye disease?

475. His anti-slavery pamphlet, *Appeal*, incited white Southerners to offer a reward for his capture in 1829.

476. In what year did Harriet Tubman escape from slavery?

477. Lincoln University, an early black college, was incorporated in 1842 under what name?

478. He claimed he was the richest black man in America in 1850.

479. In what year did Congress charter the Freedmen's Bank of Birmingham?

480. He organized the Alabama Penny Savings Bank of Birmingham in 1890.

481. In 1865, Isaac Meyers organized this company.

482. This Philadelphia African-American entered the coal business in 1865, amassing a fortune.

483. He operated a successful grocery store in 1866 in Atlanta, Georgia and accumulated $60,000.

484. In 1876, this black-owned and operated company was founded as a buggy manufacturer.

485. Where was the first black college founded?

486. He led the attack on the United States Arsenal at Harper's Ferry, Virginia in 1859.

487. This fashion designer worked with John Frederics and helped design clothes for *Gone With the Wind*.

488. Passing as a white man, he became the first black to fight for the Union Army in 1861.

489. Who was the first African-American to practice law before the Supreme Court?

490. In what year did Fisk University first open its doors?

491. What black company entered automobile manufacturing in 1900?

492. He operated one of the most popular hotels in Washington D. C.

493. He owned the street railway system and Arkansas State Fairgrounds in Pine Bluff in 1886.

494. When was the first Fourteenth Amendment, which guaranteed blacks citizenship, adopted?

495. He was the first black mayor of Newport, Rhode Island.

496. He invented a smokeless device for cooking hickory-flavored meat.

497. Who founded the National Association of Colored Women?

498. In what year did the first Pan-African Congress meet?

499. What, according to the U. S. Census of 1890, was the most common black-owned business establishment?

500. This black-owned hotel was the leading hotel in Athens, Ohio, valued at $50,000 in 1883.

501. In 1929 he was the largest shoe dealer in Pensacola, Florida.

502. Established in 1893, it was the oldest industrial insurance company operated by blacks.

503. He became president of the faltering Freedmen's Bank in 1874.

504. In 1897, this cooperative grocery store was founded in Winston, North Carolina, with capital of $10,000.

505. This case set the precedent for equalizing the salaries of black and white school teachers in 1936.

506. When was the last all-black army unit, the 24th infantry, deactivated by Congress?

507. She founded the Richmond Hospital in Virgina.

508. This black contractor invented a unique asphalt paving machine known as the Muller Paver.

509. Which black university was the first to receive a chapter of Phi Beta Kappa?

510. When did an all-black university first receive a chapter of Phi Beta Kappa?

511. What eminent African-American sociologist wrote *Black Bourgeosie?*

512. While working for Chicago's Glidden Corporation, Percy Julian extracted a soya protein used in developing the World War II fire extinguishers known by this name.

513. What black youth was brutally slain in Mississippi in 1955 for whistling at a white woman?

514. What does SCLC stand for?

515. When was the SCLC founded?

516. Who first succeeded in making the drug cortisone widely marketable at a reasonable price?

517. This slave received no credit for his role in developing the McCormick Grain Harvester alongside his master, Cyrus McCormick.

518. He invented a two-dimensional slide rule.

519. Which president awarded Medals of Freedom, the highest civilian decoration, to Ralph J. Bunche and Marian Anderson?

520. What 1964 act was responsible for such programs as Upward Bound, Head Start, and College Work-Study?

521. The largest black newspaper in 1897 was edited by whom?

522. At the turn of the century he was one of the largest brick manufacturers of the time.

523. In 1900 he owned a successful hotel in New York City worth $75,000.

524. Who became the first black certified public accountant in the United States?

525. Who has been credited with drafting Alexander Graham Bell's telephone patents?

526. Considered the most serious racial disturbance in modern American history, this riot took place in what city?.

527. Who was the first black doctor in the U. S.?

528. A. P. Albert, a Creole, invented a machine for picking this crop.

529. In what city was the Black Panther Party founded?

530. He discovered the method of preserving blood plasma,

and organized the first blood bank during World War II. ✓

531. In 1966, he became the first African-American to sit in the U.S. Senate since Reconstruction.

532. In what year was the Fair Housing Act signed?

533. He was the president of Fuller Products Co.

534. Which black inventor has been issued the greatest number of U. S. patents?

535. Who invented the potato chip?

536. What president made more appointments of blacks to high level federal posts than any previous chief executive?

537. How many top level federal appointments did President Nixon award to blacks?

538. How many black ambassadors did President Johnson appoint?

539. In what year did an African-American first become a certified public accountant?

540. When were black children first enrolled in all-white Mississippi public schools?

541. In what year did National Urban League executive, Whitney M. Young, die?

542. Who was the first black new automobile dealer in the United States?

543. In 1971, what was the only state without a black lawmaker?

544. In what year did the raid on Attica Prison take place?

545. By what name was Hyram Thomas' invention originally known?

546. When did the National Negro Finance Corporation begin?

547. How many people were killed in the raid on Attica Prison?

548. He was the first African-American to receive an NBC development contract; he was also the first black mayor of Universal City, CA.

549. This Philadelphia candymaker and confectioner is known as the "man who invented ice cream."

550. In what year were a black man and a white woman married legally for the first time in North Carolina?

551. What humanitarian organization announced a six-year, $100 million program to aid private black colleges in 1971?

552. What journalist was the first black to be elected to membership in the Gridiron Club, a prestigious organization of Washington newsmen?

553. When was the National Black Feminist Organization founded?

554. He owned a toy store at age 12.

555. For what instrument did J. H. Dickinson and S. L. Dickinson devise the machinery?

556. Who was the the first black federal judge?

557. He wrote "Carry Me Back to Ole Virginny," the state song of Virginia.

558. In what year did the Watts Riots occur?

559. In 1884, he patented a machine which made paper bags.

560. Along with Margaret Sloan, she founded the National Black Feminist Organization.

561. What did C. M. A. stand for?

562. What organization's slogan is "A Mind is a Terrible Thing to Waste?"

563. He invented thermostatically controlled air devices.

564. How many medical colleges are housed at predominantly black institutions?

565. He invented a wide range of electronic devices, among them a resistor used in many computers, radios and televisions.

566. Who is the National Representative of the Nation of Islam in Chicago, Illinois?

567. Who is credited with one of the first designs for the cutters used on aluminum foil and wax paper boxes?

568. Where is Grambling State University located?

569. In what year was the Colored Merchants Association founded?

570. He conducted a study of African-American business enterprises in 1898.

571. What Providence, Rhode Island businessman has the oldest black-owned Kentucky Fried Chicken franchise?

572. Because of his work on this Apollo 16 instrument, Dr.

George Carruthers was commended by NASA for outstanding scientific achievement.

573. In what city is Meharry Medical College located? ✓

574. During the early 1800's this city was considered "the seat of black affluence."

575. He opened a restaurant in New York City where George Washington was a frequent guest and where the New York Chamber of Commerce was organized.

576. In what city is Morehouse College located? ✓

577. This former fugitive slave opened the Inter-Ocean Hotel in 1873 in Denver.

578. Who was known as "the Negro Potato King" in Kansas during the 1880's and 1890's?

579. In 1970 he owned radio stations in Augusta, Georgia, Knoxville and Baltimore.

580. Where is Spelman College located?

581. In what city was the first black-owned bank operated?

582. He founded the Citizens Federal Savings and Loan Association and Booker T. Washington Insurance Co. Inc. of Birmingham, Alabama.

583. In 1985 this bank was the largest black-owned bank with assets of $103 million.

584. Where is Tougaloo College located?

585. Who wrote the first published study of black banks?

586. Where is Xavier University located?

587. Who refused to patent any of his agricultural innovations saying, "God gave them to me, how can I sell them to someone else?"

588. What do the letters NACW stand for?

589. Nine black youths were accused of what crime against two white women in Scottsboro, Alabama?

590. Written in 1923, this was the first published study of black banks.

591. Who was the first black philanthropist?

592. David N. Croswaithe Jr. developed the method and apparatus for heating what 70-story New York City landmark building?

593. Whom did Eleanor Roosevelt invite to the White House in defiance of her social critics?

594. Agricultural and domestic workers were not covered by what act originally?

595. Having shot down four enemy planes during the attack on Pearl Harbor, he received the Navy Cross.

596. What organization refused blood donations from African-Americans in 1941?

597. Name the first black-owned bank begun in 1888 in Richmond, VA.

598. This black woman is president of Milwaukee's Ethnic Enterprises.

599. He was issued a total of 61 patents, among them an air conditioning unit for field hospitals, a portable X-ray machine and a refrigerator for military field kitchens.

600. Where did the most destructive riot during world War II occur?

601. Where did CORE hold its first sit-in?

602. Who founded the Nation of Islam in 1934? ✓

603. In 1964, FBI agents found buried bodies of three civil rights workers in what town?

604. When did the SNCC-sponsored Selma to Montgomery march take place?

605. Who was the first African-American professional nurse?

606. He helped develop the Belzer Kidney Perfusion Machine, crucial to the process of transplanting kidneys.

607. When was the Civil Rights bill passed?

608. In what year did the first black-owned bank open?

609. In 1971, the Black Panthers split into two factions located at Oakland and what other city?

610. She became a *cause celebre* after she was charged with complicity in the death of a California Judge.

611. Dr Lloyd Tevis co-founded the first black-owned and operated hospital in what state?

612. Whose Toggle Harpoon doubled the output of the 19th century New England whaling industry?

613. W. Montague Cobb has been cited for his studies in what disciplines?

614. J. Ernest Wilkins held what position in the Eisenhower administration?

615. He was the Black National Liberty Party candidate for president in 1907?

616. What Detroit publishing company did Dudley Randall direct?

617. The first black man hired by Republic Aviation, Inc., he helped develop the first airborne radar beacon for locating downed aircraft.

618. Who was the first black mayor of New Orleans, Louisiana?

619. In 1985 this was the largest black-owned savings and loan association with assets of over $159 million.

620. In what city was the first oyster and ale establishment started in the mid 1700's by an emancipated slave named Emanuel?

621. After 1800, this African-American restauranteur opened an eating house near Wall Street.

622. Peter Augustin's catering business served this city's exclusive social circles in the mid 19th century.

623. What was the second bank organized and administered by blacks in 1888?

624. This work published by Harold Cruse in 1967 maintained that black intellectuals had opted for integrationism over nationalism.

625. What company employed Ozzie Williams in 1961 when he supervised the development and production of the control rocket systems that guided the lunar landers?

626. Who was the first black mayor of Chicago, Illinois?

627. From 1899 to 1905, how many banks were organized by African-Americans?

628. The earliest black banks were the outgrowth of what type of organizations?

629. In 1883 this prosperous grocer in Macon, Georgia was worth more than $20,000 and had more credit than any merchant in town.

630. Henry Scott founded and operated one of the most successful pickling establishments in this city prior to 1865.

631. He was Albany, New York's leading merchant tailor to 1985.

632. In 1871, this black man organized a Richmond, Virginia company which established a sassafrass oil factory.

633. Who was the first black mayor of Philadelphia, Pennsylvania?

634. In 1875 he was president of Richmond Land and Financial Association.

635. What Boston African-American had by 1880 established himself as the second largest merchant tailor in Massachusetts?

636. Who was the first black mayor of Detroit, Michigan?

637. He developed the first useful refrigeration system for trucks and railroad cars.

638. She became the first black chancellor of a predominantly white institution at the University of Colorado.

639. Who invented the Synchronous Multiplex Railway Telegraph?

640. She was the first African-American couture designer, working for such names as Henri Bendel and Neiman Marcus.

641. She was the nation's first African-American woman prosecutor.

642. Who was the first black and first woman special judge for the Second Judicial District of Mississippi?

643. What firm trained the first black member of the New York Stock Exchange as a floor partner?

644. She became the first woman and the first black Assistant Secretary at the U.S. Department of Agriculture.

645. She was Mississippi's first African-American woman mayor.

646. Who was the first woman and the first black to head a State Department Bureau with the rank of assistant secretary?

647. She was the first black woman to receive an M.D. degree in 1870.

648. Approximately how many black women doctors were there in the U.S. in 1920?

649. In what year did the New York Stock Exchange accept its first black member?

650. Approximately how many black women doctors were counted in the U.S. in 1970?

651. Who organized the National Association of Colored Graduate Nurses in 1908?

652. To whom did Garrett A. Morgan sell his 1923

patented automatic stoplight signal for $40,000?

653. An English professor at Brown University, he edited the first college guide for black students.

654. Who is the first African-American to be elected president of the National League of Cities?

655. He organized in 1919 the Black Star Line of steamships.

656. How many founders met in 1905 in Niagara Falls to draw up a platform for African-American protest?

657. African-Americans were lynched during the 1908 race riot in this city.

658. This military regiment won the *Croix de Guerre* in World War I.

659. Name the African-American cowboy who "never missed anything" and was nicknamed Deadwood Dick.

660. Chicago's black residents elected him to be the first African-American congressman since 1901--and the first elected from the North.

661. What black civil rights organization was formed in Brooklyn in June 1981?

662. Who was the first black mayor of Pasadena, California, and the first black woman to serve as mayor of an American city of 100,000 or more?

663. She became the first woman to sit on the Federal Appeals Court in Manhattan in 1979.

664. Who published *The Underground Railroad*, 800 pages of records of the Philadelphia Vigilance Committee, in 1872?

665. How many death threats did the Rev. Jesse Jackson receive when he ran for president in 1984?

666. He is the publisher of *Blackbook International Reference Guide* and *Dollars and Sense Magazine.*

667. James Weldon Jones wrote this 1930 history of blacks in New York City beginning in 1626 when the African-American population numbered 11.

668. Considered the father of black history, his two-volume *History of the Negro Race in America* was published in 1883.

669. Name the landmark 1,100 page reference of African-American biography published in 1887 by William J. Simmons.

670. Professor of Law at Georgetown University, she was head of the Equal Employment Opportunity Commission in the Carter Administration.

671. Elected as House Budget Committee chairman in 1986, this Baptist minister heads a 3,000 member church in Philadelphia.

672. This influential civil rights activist won a 1967 court case that said the placement of Washington, D.C. students on the basis of ability perpetuated segregation.

673. He became Michigan's first African-American Congressman.

674. In 1974, he became the first black state senator to seve in Alabama since Reconstruction.

675. He succeeded Andrew Young as chief American delegate to the United Nations.

676. Who authored the eloquent defense of the African-American during slavery, *The Condition of . . . the Colored*

People in 1852?

677. He was appointed president of the City University of New York in 1981.

678. This ex-slave introduced the idea of the Freedman's Memorial Monument to Abraham Lincoln in Washington, D.C. the day after his assassination.

679. After the Hamburg massacre of 1876 in South Carolina where black militia were attacked by 300 whites, this Philadelphia minister delivered the address, "How Long? How Long, O Heaven?"

680. Prinicpal of the Colored High School in Cincinnati, Ohio, he is considered the first African-American socialist.

681. The first African-American graduate of Harvard College, he was dean of Howard University's Law School from 1879 to 1880.

682. He was the first black to serve in Ohio's state senate and became known as the "Daddy of Labor Day" for introducing the state's Labor Day bill.

683. From Ottumwa, Iowa, he was the first African-American to be nominated for President of the United States in 1904.

684. Pastor of Cincinnati's New Light Baptist Church, he played a critical role during the 1950's Alabama civil rights protests.

685. President Eisenhower appointed him as the first black executive in the White House in 1955.

686. Who became the first African-American general in a line position?

687. He became the first black president of Fisk University in 1946.

688. Who was the first African-American to serve as a full delegate to the United Nations?

689. It would be 28 years before another black person was elected to Congress when he left in 1901.

690. She was the first president of the National Association of Colored Women.

691. Who was elected to the House of Representatives in 1980 after two previously unsuccessful attempts and without Chicago's "machine" endorsement?

692. She founded Bethune-Cookman College, the National Council of Negro Women and was an advisor to President Franklin D. Roosevelt.

693. Who founded the United Negro College Fund while president of Tuskegee?

694. Executive secretary of the NAACP during the key World War II growth period, he travelled to the South to investigate lynchings of blacks because he could pass for white.

695. He told the Senate Armed Services Committee in 1948 that he would urge black youths to resist the draft unless discrimination was banned.

696. Who was the first black appointed to Federal District Court in the continental United States?

697. He was the principal advocate of emigration of black Americans to Africa from Reconstructiion to World War I.

698. He became the first black congressman from the West when elected from Los Angeles in 1962.

699. When Rev. K. L. Buford and Dr. Stanley Smith were elected to a city council in 1964, they became the first African-American elected officials in the 20th century in this state.

700. John Conyers and this representative were the two black members of the House Judiciary Committee which recommended the impeachment of President Nixon.

701. This state senator was elected lieutenant governor of Colorado in 1974.

702. He was promoted to four star general and commander-in-chief of the North American Air Defense Command in 1975.

703. Named president of the Ford Foundation in 1979, he was the first black to head a major foundation.

704. Who became the first black woman elected president of the Borough of Manhattan in 1965?

705. President Johnson named him commissioner of Washington, D.C. and unofficial mayor.

706. This former aide to Martin Luther King, Jr. became the first non-voting congressional delegate from the District of Columbia since Reconstruction.

707. He headed the United Negro College Fund before his 1971 appointment as executive director of the National Urban League.

708. Name the first black state supreme court justice in the South in the 20th century, appointed in 1975.

709. Who was the first black bishop of the Washington, D.C. Episcopal diocese?

710. She was confirmed as ambassador to the Republic of

Cameroon in 1977.

711. In 1964, Tammany Hall, New York City's Democratic organization, elected this black politician as its leader.

712. How many days did the historic Selma to Montgomery march led by Martin Luther King, Jr. in 1964 last?

713. She was the first black woman ambassador, to Luxembourg, in 1965.

714. This Chicago resident was posthumously awarded the Congressional Medal of Honor for bravery in Vietnam.

715. She was the first black president of the YWCA.

716. What position did Thurgood Marshall hold before being confirmed to the Supreme Court?

717. Who was the first black woman named deputy solicitor general in 1972?

718. This black leader was elected president of the National Council of Churches in 1972.

719. The sit-in movement began in 1960 when four students from what college sat down at a lunch counter in Greensboro, N.C.?

720. She was head of the Arkansas NAACP and publisher of the *Arkansas State Press* during the 1957 school integration crisis in Little Rock, Arkansas.

721. President of Supreme Life Insurance Co. from 1955 to 1971, he had argued successfully before the Supreme Court in the 1970 *Hansberry v. Lee* case which stopped restrictive covenants.

722. A Morehouse College president for 27 years, he became the first African-American president of the Atlanta

Board of Education.

723. He became the first black to head a standing committee of Congress in 1949.

724. Name the associate press secretary to President Kennedy.

725. The first black dean of the college of Brown University, he left to become director of the Argonne National Laboratory in 1979.

726. Name the first African-American elected mayor of Pritchard, Alabama.

727. Who was the first black admiral in the U.S. Navy?

728. Who defeated Adam Clayton Powell in 1970, ending the career of one of black America's most powerful politicians?

729. Closely identified with minority business legislation, this congressman sued the University of Maryland to admit him as its first black graduate student.

730. Name the novelist who co-authored *Black Life in Corporate America* with Glegg Watson.

731. He was the first African-American to win a statewide race for executive office in North Carolina in 1978 where he served as an appeals judge.

732. He was appointed chief justice of the District of Columbia Court of Appeals in 1976.

733. This graduate of the Yale Law School was appointed commissioner and chairman of the U.S. Equal Employment Opportunity Commission by President Reagan in 1982.

734. Born in Trinidad, he was elected lieutenant governor of California in 1975 and to the House of Representatives in 1980.

735. A Morehouse College graduate, he is the only professional librarian in the House of Representatives.

736. He argued the landmark "stop and frisk" case of *Terry v. Ohio* in the United States Supreme Court in 1968.

737. This executive director of the United Negro College Fund was a legal officer with the Ford Foundation.

738. Pastor of Atlanta's Central United Methodist Church, he is president of the Southern Christian Leadership Conference.

739. This judge authored the important study of race and the American legal process, *In the Matter of Color*.

740. He was elected superintendent of public instruction for California in 1970.

741. In 1971, he was the first black mayor in the history of Tuskegee, Alabama.

742. He helped found SNCC, was its national chairman in 1960, and became the second elected mayor of the District of Columbia in 1979.

743. Who developed Soul City, the prototype new town located in Warren County, North Carolina?

744. Who authored *Black Religion and Black Radicalism*, a description of the black church's role in the development of black nationalism?

745. By the eighteenth century, this colony was the leader in the slave trade.

746. He is the author of *Blacks in Antiquity*, the story of

Africans who reached Greece and Italy.

747. President of the NAACP Legal Defense and Educational Fund, he argued the landmark *Swann v. Charlotte-Mecklenburg Board of Education*, resulting in crosstown busing.

748. Who became the first black member of Congress from Ohio in 1968?

749. Who in 1979 was named the first African-American general in the Marine Corps?

750. He was the president of the National Collegiate Athletic Association.

751. Name the first black woman president of the National Bar Association.

752. This journalist became the majority shareholder in the corporation that purchased the Oakland, California *Tribune* newspaper in 1982

753. Whose release did Rev. Jesse Jackson negotiate after this lieutenant was shot down over Lebanon in 1984?

754. In 1855, he became the first black elected to public office in the country when he won the post of township clerk in Brownhelm, Ohio.

755. To what did the National Negro Committee change its name?

ART AND LITERATURE

Above (l. to r.): Louis Latimer; Charles Johnson; W.E.B. DuBois; Dr. Martin Luther King, Jr. *Below* (l. to r.): Duke Ellington; Paul Robeson.

ART AND LITERATURE

756. Who was called "the poet laureate of the Negro race"?

757. In 1965 he published *Manchild in the Promised Land.*

758. What black landscape painter helped George Whitaker and Charles Stetson found the Providence Art Club in 1880?

759. What landscape by Edward Bannister won a first award medal at the Centennial Exhibition in Philadelphia and sold for $1,500?

760. What sculptress left Oberlin at the age of fifteen, having been charged with poisoning two of her white schoolmates with an aphrodisiac?

761. Carlene Hatcher Polite was one of the first black women writers to address turbulence in relationships between black men and women in this 1967 novel.

762. Having been encouraged by Thomas Eakins to paint genre scenes, he executed *The Banjo Lesson* in 1893.

763. After winning a gold medal for the *Resurrection of Lazarus* at the Salon of 1897, this painter was designated chevalier of the French Legion of Honor in 1923.

764. At the end of this controversial book published in 1979, Michelle Wallace warns black women not to blame black men for their own oppression.

765. Richmond Barthé's subject for this full-figure sculpture was Rose McClendon playing Serena in *Porgy.*

766. This black novelist wrote *Eva's Man,* in which the heroine castrates her dead lover with her teeth, and *Corregidora,* the story of a woman who loses her baby after her husband has thrown her down the stairs.

767. His 1760 poem, "An Evening Thought: Salvation by Christ and Penitential Cries," is the earliest known work published by an African-American.

768. How many novels do we know of that were published by blacks before 1890?

769. Charles Waddell Chestnutt, a turn-of-the-century author renowned for his short stories, published a biography of what famous African-American?

770. What 1874 book by a former slave reached its eighth edition in London only five years after publication?

771. After he had published his *Appeal* in 1829, a reward of $10,000 was placed on his head.

772. Having sculpted *Le Pecheur* and *Le Baiser* in New Orleans, he sailed to Europe in 1852.

773. What is Langston Hughes' first autobiography called?

774. For what 1927 work is James Weldon Johnson well known?

775. Jean Toomer published this important collection of poetry and prose in 1932.

776. What romantic poet published *Not a Man and Yet a Man* (1877) and *The Rape of Florida* (1884)?

777. This "black protest" novel by Richard Wright became an immediate bestseller in 1940.

778. Who wrote *Go Tell It On the Mountain* while living in Paris?

779. What groundbreaking 1952 novel by Ralph Ellison chronicles the life of a Southern black man who cannot escape racism in the North?

780. Who is the main character of John A. Williams' 1967 novel, *The Man Who Cried I Am*?

781. Author of the 1964 Obie Award play, *The Dutchman*, he later changed his name from LeRoi Jones.

782. A colonial slave, he is the first known American black to have received formal training as an artist.

783. Eighteenth century slaves in New Orleans excelled at what trade?

784. Painter Edward M. Bannister was born here in 1828.

785. Having seen his mural *The Lotus Eaters*, Lord Alfred Tennyson invited this artist to his home on the Isle of Wight.

786. Grants from this federal project supported blacks in depicting their history and culture in murals.

787. She journeyed to Paris on the proceeds from a bust of Colonel Robert Gould Shaw sculpted from a photograph.

788. His 1945 autobiography, *Black Boy* has become a standard text in American high schools.

789. This organization has been exhibiting the works of black artists since 1928, and probably now possesses the largest collection in the United States.

790. What famous black woodblock artist went to Atlanta University as a professor in 1939 and helped other black artists gain recognition?

791. What university counts among its graduates painters Mildred Thompson and William White?

792. Who is the best-known black primitive painter?

793. What black primitivist, whose right arm was paralyzed by a sniper, painted images from World War I?

794. What is the name of the group of black printmakers centered at Atlanta University in the late 1930's?

795. What black abstract expressionist painted creatures that resembled bats and human beings?

796. Jack Whitten, Larry Compton, Sonny Hodge and Joe Overstreet all belong to what school of painters?

797. From what country was poet Phillis Wheatley taken in 1761?

798. Which black artist of the Depression restricted himself to church murals?

799. She published "A Poem by Phillis, A Negro Girl in Boston, on the Death of the Reverend George Whitefield" at the age of seventeen.

800. In what city did Phillis Wheatley publish *Poems on*

Various Subjects: Religious and Moral in 1773?

801. What black artist headed the department of art at Howard University and published *Modern Negro Art* in 1943?

802. In what city was *Les Cenelles*, the first black American anthology of poetry, compiled in 1845?

803. Having worked as an elevator operator for four dollars weekly, he achieved fame upon publication of *Lyrics of Lowly Life* in 1896.

804. This black woman, while still in her twenties. was renowned for the neo-classical sculptures she was producing in Rome in the 19th century.

805. Who published the poem, "The Harlem Dancer" under the pen name, Eli Edwards in 1917?

806. Elizabeth Keckley, author of *Behind the Scenes; or, Thirty Years a Slave, and Four Years in the White House,* was a designer for whom during the Civil War?

807. "The Goophered Grapevine," Charles Waddell Chestnutt's first published short story, was later included in what collection of his works?

808. He wrote, "I am certain that while we are slaves, it is our duty to obey our masters in all their lawful commands," in the early 19th century.

809. From what 1845 work are the following words taken: "It was not *color,* but *crime,* not *God,* but *man,* that afforded the true explanation of the existence of slavery?

810. The first play and the first two novels to be published by an African-American were written by what abolitionist?

811. Who published *Up From Slavery, a Narrative* in 1900?

812. In this 1902 novel by Paul Lawrence Dunbar, most of the characters are black.

813. Better known for his murals, he painted *La Pauvre Voisine,* which was exhibited at the Salon of 1912 in Paris and later sold to the Argentine government for $600.

814. This black woman wrote *Men and Mules* and *Their Eyes Were Watching God* during the Depression.

815. Funds from what federal project helped support Richard Wright and Ralph Ellison?

816. He authored *Nobody Knows My Name* and *The Fire Next Time.*

817. What play by ntozake shange features seven black women, each from a different city and each named after a color?

818. What is the nickname of Macon Dead III, the main character in Toni Morrison's novel, *Song of Solomon?*

819. Best known as a critic of American poetry, this black writer's own first collection of poems is titled *Lyrics of Life and Love.*

820. This author collaborated with his brother, a musician, to write the song, "Lift Ev'ry Voice and Sing."

821. What collection published by Chandler Harris in 1880 made the black oral tradition available to all Americans?

822. He is a character in five of Langston Hughes' books.

823. In 1746, at the age of sixteen, she wrote "Bars Fight," the first known piece of literature written by a black.

824. Poet Paul Lawrence Dunbar was what black writer's

first husband?

825. In what 1916 work does George Reginald Margetson detail the political education of a young poet?

826. One of the first black protest poets and author of *Hope of Liberty*, he gained access to the English classics when his master lent him out as a janitor to the University of North Carolina.

827. The author of *America and Other Poems*, he felt that the colonization of Central America by blacks was their best route to freedom.

828. Frances Ellen Watkins Harper, active in the causes of abolition, womens' rights, and temperance, published what volume in 1854?

829. What folk character outwitted a wolf, a bear and a fox in stories that whites did not suspect were about slaves and slavemasters?

830. From what black's autobiography is Harriet Beecher Stowe thought to have lifted the character of Uncle Tom?

831. William Wells Brown based his first novel, *Clotel; or, The President's Daughter*, on which president?

832. A physician, he published *The Conjure Woman* in 1932, and short stories in the *Atlantic Monthly*.

833. He wrote *The Garies and Their Friends*, the first black novel to describe ethnic prejudice against blacks in the North.

834. What African animal became the fox in black American folk tales?

835. What Harvard-educated doctor supported the colonization of Central America by blacks?

836. What black lawyer and short story writer hid his racial identity from the *Atlantic Monthly* for almost ten years?

837. Who termed the Northern black upper class the "talented tenth"?

838. Her novel, *Iola Leroy, or Shadows Uplifted (1892),* was the second to be published by a black American woman.

839. In what 1912 novel does James Weldon Johnson deal with a mulatto man's indecision over whether or not to sacrifice his identity as a black for social advancement?

840. In what collection of essays does W.E.B. DuBois' famous essay, "The Sorrow Songs" appear?

841. Eric Walrond based this 1926 collection of stories on his experience among poor blacks in the West Indies.

842. What white writer made blacks the subject of his plays, *The Emperor Jones* and *All God's Chillun Got Wings?*

843. Who is the main character of Claude McKay's 1928 bestseller, *Home to Harlem?*

844. His first collection of poems, *Southern Road,* was published in 1932.

845. What 1928 novel by Nella Larsen features Helga Crane, a 23-old mulatto searching for a place in American society?

846. In what country is a slave insurrection about to occur in Martin R. Delany's *Blake,* the third novel published by a black?

847. In what satirical novel by George S. Schuyler does an electrical process convert blacks into whites, the end result being that blacks are now whiter than whites and racism is reversed?

848. Arna Bontemps based his 1936 novel, *Black Thunder,* on whose 1800 attempted slave revolt?

849. Who began her studies of black folklore under Franz Boaz at Barnard College, and learned about voodooism on her own in New Orleans?

850. The painter of *Chicken Shack,* he held the first one-man show by a black since Henry Tanner, at the New Gallery in New York in 1928.

851. Countée Cullen's *Color,* Claude McKay's *Harlem Shadows,* and W.E.B. DuBois' *The Gift of Black Folk* were all published in this year.

852. Known best for his four murals at the Schomburg Center for Black Culture in New York, he illustrated James Weldon Johnson's *God's Trombones* and much of Alain Locke's *The New Negro* in 1925.

853. In what country did the painter William H. Johnson choose to settle for years?

854. He won the Otto H. Kahn prize at the 1928 Harmon exhibit for his painting, *Swing Low, Sweet Chariot.*

855. This Harlem Renaissance artist of black, French and Indian descent has sculpted many important black figures, including Booker T. Washington and Toussaint L'Ouverture.

856. Recipient of the Harmon bronze award in fine arts in 1929, he sculpted *Pearl* and *Chester.*

857. The first black editor of Brown University's student daily, Wallace Terry wrote this Pulitzer Prize-nominated book about black veterans.

858. This black woman was a professor of fine arts at Howard University for 45 years, and exhibited her impressionist works at the Vose Gallery in Boston in 1938.

859. How old was Alma W. Thomas when she had a one-woman show at the Whitney Museum and a retrospective at the Corcoran Gallery?

860. In what 1959 play by Lorraine Hansberry does the Younger family inherit $10,000 from an insurance policy?

861. She is the first black woman to have her film script produced with the movie, *Georgia, Georgia* in 1972.

862. How old was Gwendolyn Brooks when she published her first poem, "Eventide?"

863. What famous poet of the black experience published conversations that she had had with James Baldwin in 1973, and Margaret Walker in 1974?

864. Her first novel was *The Third Life of Grange Copeland*, published in 1970.

865. In 1976, he was the first African-American to become Poetry Consultant for the Library of Congress.

866. Who was the first black woman to win the National Book Critics Circle Award in 1977?

867. What is the name of Maya Angelou's fourth autobiographical work, written in 1981?

868. What black woman published *Gorilla, My Love*, a 1972 collection of short stories narrated by a black girl?

869. What black poet wrote the lines, "Nigger/Can you kill/Can you kill?"

870. This 1973 book about the ghetto by Alexis Deveaux

contains her surrealistic drawings along with narrative, dialogue and lyric.

871. Elgar Enders, a rich white man who purchases a tenement house in a black ghetto, is the hero of what 1966 novel by Kristin Hunter?

872. What 1980 book by poet Audre Lorde details her struggle with cancer?

873. A graduate of Brown University, her 1977 collection of short stories, *White Rat,* is about blacks in rural Kentucky.

874. This 1969 novel by Toni Morrison is about Pecola Breedlove, a black girl who wishes she looked like Shirley Temple.

875. What black woman poet, playwright, novelist and educator wrote *The Adventures of Small Head, Square Head and Fathead* in 1973?

876. In defiance of the tyranny of American culture over black women, novelist Paulette Williams choose what Zulu name for herself?

877. In 1964 he published *Catherine Carmier,* his first novel which describes the cultural alienation of a black man returning to the South.

878. Who received the 1942 Yale Younger Poets Award for the collection, *For My People?*

879. In what 1975 collection does Sherley Anne Williams address the theme of black women and the blues?

880. What 1948 novel by Dorothy West deals with the Northern black bourgeoisie?

881. In what 1965 novel by William Demby does the

author himself become a character writing in Rome?

882. Arna Bontemps' historical novel, *Dreams at Dusk,* is based on the Haitian slave revolt led by what man?

883. Who won the Iowa School of Letters Award for Short Fiction for *The Beach Umbrella,* his first book, at the age of 60?

884. Separate But Equal, this black artist's statement on the nineteenth-century slave trade, was the first exhibition held at New York's Cinque Gallery, in 1969.

885 What verse drama by Owen Dodson tells us not to wait for Christ to save us?

886. What important black novelist finds the roots of all American literature in racial conflict in his essay, "Twentieth-Century Fiction and the Black Mask of Humanity"?

887. This novel by Ernest J. Gaines became a successful television film starring Cicely Tyson.

888. What 1982 novel by ntozake shange contains no punctuation?

889. Michael Harper, who published *Dear John, Dear Coltrane* in 1970, was pursuing what degree when he decided to become a poet?

890. In his poem, "John Brown's Body," he laments the fact that only in years to come will poets be able to write about the "black spear."

891. In which of Clarence Major's novels must Eli Bolton search for meaning and identity in a world of chaos?

892. Margaret Walker published her first poem in this magazine.

893. What black writer, who co-authored and co-starred with Ruby Dee in the movie *Up Tight,* started *The African Review* in 1962?

894. Who wrote *The Long Night* (1951), *The Grand Parade* (1961), and *The Hit* (1967)?

895. Whose body is being buried in Ishmael Reed's 1967 novel, *The Free-Lance Pallbearers* ?

896. Who wrote *Captain Blackman,* the story of a Vietnam soldier's struggle?

897. Lester Jefferson buys a wig in this 1966 novel by Charles Wright because the salesman has told him that it will allow him to fit into society.

898. What black poet published *Dancing* and *The Song Turning Back Into Itself?*

899. Which of James Baldwin's first two novels deals with homosexual love?

900. Who is the main character of Gwendolyn Brooks' first and only novel?

901. He won the Grand Prize for Poetry at the First World African Festival of Arts for his 1965 collection, *A Ballad of Remembrance.*

902. Margaret Walker presented this 1966 novel for her Ph.D. dissertation at the University of Iowa.

903. Nicodemus, Ladykiller, Nat Turner, the Boys, the Inspector, June Bug and Moses are all names given to the narrator of *NO,* the second novel by this writer.

904. She travelled throughout the West Indies and rediscovered the culture of her ancestors before publishing

Brown Girl, Brownstones in 1959.

905. To whom did Phillis Wheatley dedicate her 1773 poem, *To S.M., A Young African Painter On Seeing His Works?*

906. What black playwright married publisher Robert Nemiroff in 1953?

907. What black satirist studied under Archibald MacLeish and John Hawkes, and published *A Different Drummer* in 1962?

908. Her sculpture, *The Wretched*, exhibited at the Paris Salon of 1903, won praise from Auguste Rodin.

909. A sculptress concerned with the position of the mulatto, she is also known for her portrait busts of Paul Lawrence Dunbar, W.E.B. DuBois and Francis Grimké.

910. This white artist painted *The Gulf Stream*, a work of major importance in the breakdown of stereotyped portrayals of blacks in art.

911. What black artist and teacher sculpted *African Savage* and *Tom Tom?*

912. Eldzier Cortor, a graduate of the Art Institute of Chicago and painter of *Slum Song* (1962), was an easel painter for this organization in 1937.

913. The Rev. G.W. Hobbs' 1785 pastel of this political leader is considered to be the first portrait of a black by another black.

914. Who was the first African-American to be recognized as a portrait painter?

915. His is the only known self-portrait by a colonial black.

916. Where is Metoyer House, the oldest home in America known to have been constructed by and for blacks?

917. Robert M. Douglass Jr. sold his lithographs of this man in 1833 at fifty cents a copy for the abolitionist cause.

918. Whose engraving captioned, "Am I not a man and a brother?" became the emblem of the antislavery movement in Britain?

919. A cousin of Frederick Douglass, he is thought to have executed a portrait of Abraham Lincoln which the president commissioned himself.

920. William Simpson, the black abolitionist who executed the Loguen portraits in 1835, was first recognized by what black writer?

921. Robert Stuart Duncanson's 1853 painting, *Uncle Tom and Little Eva,* is an illustration for what book?

922. A lithographer in the 1850's, Grafton Tyler Brown is recognized as the first black artist to have worked in this state.

923. He painted *Grand Canyon of the Yellow-Stone from Hayden Point* in 1891.

924. What sculpture by Meta Warrick Fuller portrays a woman freeing herself from mummy-like bands of cloth?

925. Although he won critical acclaim in Boston for his portrait of Lizzie May Ulmer in 1776, he had difficulty obtaining commissions.

926. In 1939, who sculpted two eight-foot figures seated on llamas?

927. What is Edmonia Lewis' Chippewa name?

928. Although he died at 37, this black painter was aware of modern artistic trends, particularly of the Barbizon School in France, and received much critical acclaim.

929. Having studied from 1924 to 1925 at l'Acadèmie de la Grande Chaumiére in Paris, portraits of hers such as *Frankie* (1937) took on a Romantic aspect.

930. Having developed an interest in black subject matter while studying in France, Palmer Hayden painted a series of 12 scenes from the life of this black folk hero between 1944 and 1954.

931. The son of a black artist, he was fascinated with Haiti, and exhibits expressionist and realist tendencies in paintings such as *Bird Vendor.*

932. Famous for his 1933 piece in laquered cloth over wood, *Forever Free,* he married the sculptress May Howard Jackson.

933. Citizens of San Francisco's Chinatown helped this painter out of his financial difficulties, and he painted *Oriental Child* there in 1900.

934. He left Florence, North Carolina for fourteen years after having been jailed for using a brothel, the Jacobia Hotel, as the subject of a painting in 1930.

935. What African-American artist whose woodcuts include *African Fantasy* (1929) was also an innovative teacher of art?

936. This abstract expressionist, whose brother was also a painter, was happy to receive portrait commissions from public figures such as Henry Miller, Marian Anderson and Al Hirschfeld.

937. What group founded in 1963 by Romare Bearden and Norman Lewis asserted that it would paint only in black and white, in order to address racial conflict?

938. At what university was the first major black art gallery established?

939. This sculptor received much media attention but preferred not to discuss his aims with interviewers, instead letting works such as *Supplication* speak for themselves.

940. Trained at Columbia University as well as in Paris and Vienna, her 1972 alabaster sculpture, *Peace* is among her best works.

941. Until he won a solo exhibition at the Museum of Modern Art in 1938, William Edmonson supported himself by painting these.

942. His 1949 mural for the black role in the settlement of California, *Exploration and Colonization,* is adjacent to Hale Woodruff's *Settlement and Development* in Los Angeles.

943. What 1937 mural by Charles Alston is in the Harlem Hospital?

944. He studied with Augusta Savage, and painted such diverse works as *Yellow Hat* (1940) and *Processional* (1965).

945. His experimentation with photography in collages is represented by *The Prevalence of Ritual: Tidings* (1967).

946. Where in New York City did Joseph Delaney take a painting class with Jackson Pollock during the Depression?

947. Visits to this sculptress' studio allowed Jacob Lawrence to meet important figures of the Harlem Renaissance, including Claude McKay, Aaron Douglas, Alain Locke, and Countée Cullen.

948. Who said of his 1940-41 series, *The Migration of the Negro,* "The black man in America is always trying to better his condition and the conditions of his children."?

949. What 1943 mural by Charles White features Crispus Attucks, Denmark Vesey, Booker T. Washington and George Washington Carver, among others?

950. Active in the civil rights movement, she counts among her works the cedar sculpture, *Black Unity* (1968), and the lithograph, *Negro es Bello* (1968).

951. *Roz* (1972), and *Trabajadores* (1973), are representative of the social expression in this black painter and printmaker's work.

952. What 'sixties group claimed as its philosophy "Black Art -- for Black People"?

953. Herman ("Kofi") Bailey, who painted *Unity* in mixed media in 1961, received most of his artistic influence from what continent?

954. After visiting Africa in 1970, he produced a series on the country in red pencil, one of which, *Page From an African Notebook,* integrates human profiles and figures into the patterns of African fabric.

955. Paintings such as *Natural Woman* (1972), with its strong captivating color and the mixing of black profiles into abstract patterning, reflect the influence of Africa on this African-American artist.

956. His ink, paint and graphite work, *One Common Thought* (1972), refers to the circular eye, a symbolic element in African sculpture.

957. Paul Keene's 1969 painting, *Garden of Shango,* represents which ancient Yoruba diety?

958. The black madonna and child in this black artist's 1971 acrylic painting *Guardian?* are protected by an ankh, a black liberation flag, the African continent and a jackal.

959. In reference to the subjects of her 1974 painting *Gossip in the Sanctuary*, she says, "In church, they felt free to dream, to hope, and to show all the human instincts..."

960. Reginald Gammon's 1970 painting, *Scottsboro Mothers*, depicts the mothers of a real-life group of black men who were charged with what crime?

961. What black feminist created the mixed-media *Family of Women* series in the 1970's?

962. What object have black painters Cliff Joseph, David Bradford, Bertrand Phillips, Manuel Hughes, Phillip Lindsay Mason and Dana Chandler all used to symbolize their anger at social injustice?

963. William Walker, Mitchell Caton and Eugene Eda have all been involved in producing collective street murals in what city?

964. Where is the African-American mural, *Wall of Respect?*

965. This black sculptress, who dedicated her first one-woman show to Malcolm X, has lived in Paris since 1961.

966. Hughie Lee-Smith and Charles Sallee are both graduates of what black art school in Cleveland?

967. What twentieth century creator from St. Thomas tried to fuse poetry, music and art in his paintings for the *Blues for Nat Turner Jazz Suite?*

968. In his 1778 painting, *Watson and the Shark*, this white artist placed a black figure in a heroic position beside whites.

969. What white artist painted *Both Members of the Club*

(1909), the subject of which is a black and a white boxer "trying to beat each others brains out for money"?

970. He organized the first large-scale exhibition of African American art in New York City in 1862.

971. The aim of this art school founded by Russell and Rowena Jeliffe in Cleveland in 1915 was to put blacks on an equal creative footing with whites, and to allow them to convey their unique experiences through art.

972. Sculptress Barbara Chase-Riboud won an award for one of her prints from this magazine at 15; it was later sold to the Museum of Modern Art.

973. Henry Gudgel, son of a white man and a black slave, carved what object reminiscent of African art for Union soldier John Bryan in 1863?

974. His *Early Afternoon at Montigny* won a thirty-dollar prize for "most worthy landscape shown" at the Art Institute of Chicago's 1905 exhibition.

975. Aaron Douglas helped collect African-American art to illustrate what notable Harlem Renaissance publication?

976. The works of African-Americans were not included in this 1935 exhibition of violence towards Southern blacks.

977. Who organized the 1941 exhibition, "Afro-American Art on Both Continents," which included the works of Romare Bearden and the Delaney brothers?

978. Eldzier Cortor, Lois Mailou Jones, Jacob Lawrence and Hughie Lee-Smith all participated in the Chicago exhibition "Art of the American Negro" in what year?

979. How many black artists had one-man shows between World War II and 1954?

980. This black printer from Knoxville, Tenn. defended his decision to live abroad in 1956: "Expatriate?...One must belong before one may then not belong. I am able to realize myself here. I am no expatriate."

981. He became interested in art at 40, when he met his wife Jeanne Reynal, also an artist; fourteen years later (1970), his paintings were in the permanent collections of most major American museums.

982. After meeting black artists like Archibald Motley, Gwendolyn Brooks and Richard Wright in the Chicago studio of dancer Katherine Dunham, he helped George Neal form the Arts and Crafts Guild.

983. She produced figures such as *Mrs. Jackson* (1968), a carved and painted slab of plywood wearing real clothes.

984. What neighborhood museum in Washington, D.C. associated with the Smithsonian Institution features the art of African-Americans?

985. Where is the National Center of Afro-American Art?

986. In what year were the Museum of African Art and the Frederick Douglass Institute in Washington, D.C. founded?

987. What important exhibition was held at the Studio Museum to protest the Whitney Museum's exclusion of black artists from its show of works from the Depression?

988. What group of artists in Harlem organized to locate their roots in African art?

989. Tom Lloyd founded this innovative museum of black history and culture in Jamaica, New York.

990. Norman Lewis, Romare Bearden and Ernest Crichlow founded what showroom for young minority artists in Manhattan's East Village?

991. What Philadelphia museum was named after the African "City of the Gods?"

992. This Chicago community organization was set up to help blacks learn through art.

993. Topper Carew founded this Washington, D.C. center for art education and alternative high school for blacks.

994. What Metropolitan Museum of Art exhibition was the Black Emergency Cultural Coalition unhappy with when they picketed the museum in 1969?

995. What San Francisco Gallery was organized in 1967 by a group of street artists?

996. Considered the most important black art exhibit of the mid-'sixties, this New York show was organized by Romare Bearden and Carroll Greene, Jr..

997. In what city did Dana Chandler and Gary Rickson paint their Black Power mural next to a playground?

998. Where is the *Wall of Dignity?*

999. Charles White, who said, "Paint is the only weapon I have in which to fight what I resent," was influenced by the muralists of what country?

1000. The murals *Black Music* and *Black Leaders* hang in a cafeteria of what college?

1001. What 1970 painting by Dana Chandler is dedicated to a slain Black Panther leader?

1002. What black artist produced works like *Pray for America* (1969) by covering himself with margarine?

1003. Black Emergency Cultural Coalition leaders Joseph

and Benny Andrews wrote to Governor Nelson Rockefeller in 1971 to request funding for an art program at what institution?

1004. In her 1976 memoir, *Generations,* she tells of how her great-grandmother was hanged for having murdered her white lover

1005. In what year was the "Judson Three" convicted of desecrating the American flag on their canvases?

1006. What poet published *Black Boogaloo* (1969) and *Hoodoo Hollerin' Bebop Ghosts* (1975)?

1007. This artist of African and American Indian descent, who has painted such abstract landscapes as *The Gorge* (1966), is also a jazz singer.

1008. The engraver of *David in the Wilderness* (1955-6), her works are included in the permanent collections of museums in Washington, New York, Scotland and England.

1009. A black sculptor who combines art with technology, he was the first artist-in-residence at the Studio Museum in Harlem.

1010. His works, among them *A Fine and Secret Place* (1967), and *Little Boys Are Very Impressionable* (1967), attach evocative words to abstract images.

1011. How old was Richard Hunt when he sold his sculpture, *Arachne,* to the Museum of Modern Art in 1956?

1012. What is the geometric shape of Betty Blayton's large-scale 1970 oil collages *Concentrated Energies* and *Iconograph?*

1013. William T. Williams, who executed the series of four pencil drawings, *The Evolution of the NIGGER,* links his first racial awareness to contact with what group of people living near his home in Cross Creek, North Carolina?

1014. What 1965 collage by Alvin Hollingsworth is a black variation on one of Picasso's works?

1015. On what 1965 events did black painter Merton B. Simpson base his *Confrontation* series?

1016. Painter Benny Andrews designed album covers for this record company.

1017. How old was Joe Overstreet when he and his family moved from Mississippi to California and he began painting?

1018. This black artist printed a pamphlet called *Black is a Color.*

1019. Much of the wire and chain components of Mel Edwards' "lynch fragments" at his 1970 Whitney Museum show came from the rubble that was left over from what Chicago events?

1020. What 1963 tragedy in Birmingham, Alabama was Daniel Larue Johnson protesting when he constructed *Yesterday*, a three-dimensional box containing a headless doll with her hand caught in a mousetrap next to an American flag?

1021. What black artist has produced life-sized body parts with African designs on them such as *Black Leg* (1969)?

1022. Who was the first president of the Boston Negro Artist Association and cultural chairman of the Malcolm X Foundation?

1023. What rusty metal object did Lovett Thompson push through the neck of his 1970 wood carving, *The Junkie?*

1024. How many pages of Robert Dean Pharr's 400+ page first novel, *The Book of Numbers* (1969), contain white characters?

1025. In what public institutions did poet Etheridge Knight receive eight years of schooling?

1026. How old was Amiri Baraka (LeRoi Jones) when he graduated from Howard University?

1027. What painting by Henry Ossawa Tanner hangs in the Luxembourg Museum in Paris?

1028. What is the subject of Meta Vaux Warrick Fuller's first clay work?

1029. In 1903-4 Pauline Hopkins was editor of this Boston magazine which subscribed to the philosophy of Booker T. Washington.

1030. He wrote *By Sanction of Law,* a melodramatic novel about members of the black bourgeoisie, in 1924.

1031. Both Bryant Rollins' 1967 *Danger Song* and Dorothy West's 1948 *The Living Is Easy* are situated in what neighborhood?

1032. In what institution did Chester Himes witness a fire that killed 320 people and inspired his 1934 short story, "To What Red Hell?"

1033. Black poets Angelina Grimké and Anne Spencer were both published for the first time in this anthology edited by Countée Cullen.

1034. This black writer became a popular novelist in the 1940's, but he never mentioned blacks in his works.

1035. How many black authors did Chester Eisinger include in his 1963 anthology, *Fiction of the Forties?*

1036. What black poet was elected mayor of Langston,

Oklahoma four times?

1037. Having won the encouragement of Richard Wright while studying at the Sorbonne, he published his first volume of poetry under the pen name Paul Vesey in Germany in 1956.

1038. During what decade did the black militant Broadside Poets write?

1039. In her poem "Black Jam for Dr. Negro", she attacks the black middle class.

1040. The title of black poet Conrad Kent Rivers' poem, "By African Moonlight on Forgotten Shores" refers to the death of what black figure?

1041. What black librarian, writer, and translator of Russian and French started Broadside Press in 1965?

1042. Before he was thirty, Haki Madhubuti had published four volumes of poetry under this original name.

1043. A contributor to Frederick Douglass' *North Star* and author of *Autobiography of A Fugitive Slave (1855)*, he moved from New York to Canada in 1851 to escape the fugitive slave laws.

1044. He anticipated the Harlem Renaissance in poetic collections like *Visions of the Dusk (1915)* and *Songs of the Soil (1916)*.

1045. Writer Jean Toomer was born into the mulatto elite in what city?

1046. Who published *Stranger and Alone* in 1950?

1047. In this 1964 novel, his first, John O. Killens traces a black family in Georgia through two generations.

1048. Once an assistant editor of *Poetry* magazine, she co-authored *Poem: Counterpoem* with Dudley Randall.

1049. What volume of poetry did Mari Evans publish in 1970?

1050. Whose autobiography, *Report From Part One,* was published in 1972?

1051. What kinds of writers are collected in the anthologies *Sturdy Black Bridges, Confirmation, Black Eyed Susans* and *Midnight Birds?*

1052. This 1972 book by Albert Murray describes a black man's encounters with blacks and whites on a journey from Harlem to Alabama.

1053. He is recognized for his critical works, the most important of which is *The Way of the New World: the Black Novel in America* (1975).

1054. What anthology of the Black Arts Movement did Amiri Baraka and Larry Neal co-edit in 1968?

1055. What poet published *The Black Unicorn* in 1978?

1056. In addition to authoring several books for young people and working with poetry and film, she published a biography of Fannie Lou Hamer in 1972.

1057. What African-American from Detroit founded the Yoruba Temple in Harlem in 1960 and helped stimulate the utilization of Yoruba tradition among New York artists?

1058. What black novelist of the bourgeois tradition was literary editor for the NAACP's *Crisis* magazine under W.E.B. DuBois?

1059. She published *Sarah Phillips,* the story of an upper-middle-class adolescent whose struggles to separate herself from her black race are ultimately successful.

1060. This 1969 children's book by Kristin Hunter deals with Louretta Hawkins' quest for self while growing up in the ghetto.

1061. David Bradley won a PEN/Faulkner award in 1982 for this novel.

1062. Who is the subject of black sculptor John Wilson's 1985 bust which was the first portrait of a black man to be installed in the Capitol in Washington, D.C.?

1063. What drama about the murder of a psychotic black Army seargent won Charles H. Fuller, Jr. the Pulitzer Prize in 1982, and has since become a major motion picture?

1064. This important black sculptor is thought to have derived some of his ideas from a six-year stint working in the University of Chicago's zoological experimental laboratory.

1065. While serving time in the Ohio State Penitentiary between 1928 and 1936 for armed robbery, he published short stories in *Esquire, Coronet, Abbott's Monthly Magazine,* and *The Bronzeman.*

1066. Melvin B. Tolson, author of *Harlem Gallery (1965),* was poet laureate of this African nation which had originally served as a refuge for ex-slaves and free blacks.

1067. Black poets Dudley Randall and Margaret Danner both worked at this Detroit cultural center in the early 1960's.

1068. Charles L. Reason, George B. Vashon and James Madison Bell all wrote poetry for what cause?

1069. In this, John Wideman's third novel, Philadelphia blacks plot the lynching of a white policeman.

1070. Alice Childress was made Honorary Citizen of Atlanta when this, her play about interracial love, opened there in 1975.

1071. He won an Obie for *The Fabulous Miss Marie* in 1975.

1072. In 1965, he was recruited by Harvard Law School and his second short story, "Gold Coast," was awarded first prize by *The Atlantic Monthly*.

1073. Author of the 1974 collection of poems, *An Ordinary Woman,* she has also written sixteen books for children.

1074. Poet Victor Hernàndez Cruz edited this 1960's periodical published by a black artists' collective on New York's Lower East Side.

1075. In 1970 his sixth volume of poetry, *Words in the Mourning Time,* was nominated for the National Book Award.

1076. His 1837 narrative details how his white father's wife, upon learning that he was the son of her husband and one of her slaves, attempted to kill him with a knife and a club.

1077. In her *Journal,* Charlotte Forten Grimké, later the wife of the Rev. Francis Grimké, narrates her two successful years educating ex-slaves in what region captured by the Union army?

1078. In 1890 she wrote *Clarence and Chlorine, or God's Way* one of the few black novels popular at this time.

1079. He is considered to be the first African-American to have written poetry in black plantation dialect.

1080. A dramatist and short story writer as well, he

published three volumes of poetry: *A Little Dreaming (1913)*, *Visions of Dusk (1915)*, and *Songs of the Soil (1916)*.

1081. After 1922, this black journalist and fiction writer from Georgetown, British Guyana published in numerous periodicals, among them *The New Republic*, *Opportunity*, *Vanity Fair*, *The Saturday Review of Literature*, *Argosy All-Story Magazine*, and *Current History*.

1082. What black periodical of the arts, which lasted only one issue in the twenties, contained the works of Zora Neale Hurston, Aaron Douglas, John P. Davis, Gwendolyn Bennett, Bruce Nugent and Langston Hughes?

1083. Besides being a movie director, composer, author and semi-pro basketball player, he was a photographer for *Life* magazine from 1948 to 1972.

1084. "Three Fightingmen," a bronze statue of two white soldiers and one black, was installed at what U.S. memorial in 1984?

1085. What African-American novelist won the Pulitzer Prize and the American Book Award in 1983?

1086. Paule Marshall won the 1984 American Book Award for this novel.

1087. She won the 1983 American Book Award for First Fiction for her novel, *Women of Brewster Place*.

1088. Her novel, *The Street*, was published in 1946.

1089. In what critically acclaimed 1972 novel by Barry Beckham does Henry Adams experience "daymares"?

1090. Best known for his 1969 novel, *The Life and Loves of Mr. Jiveass Nigger*, he attacks the racial stereotyping of blacks by white authors and filmmakers in his writing.

1091. Hal Bennett was named most promising writer of 1970 for his short story, "Dotson Gerber Resurrected" by what magazine?

1092. He started out as a feature writer for the *Newark Herald News* at sixteen, published *A Wilderness of Vines*, his first novel, in 1966, and won the Faulkner Award in 1973.

1093. Internationally acclaimed sculptress Barbara Chase-Riboud based what 1979 historical novel on Thomas Jefferson's life?

1094. Which of Ronald L. Fair's novels won a Best Book Award from the American Library Association in 1972?

1095. Author of *There Is a Tree More Ancient Than Eden (1973)*, he combines religious and secular symbols in images such as that of a switchblade being used to serve the bread of the Eucharist.

1096. This 1970 novel by Louise Meriwether tells the story of a twelve-year-old girl in Harlem during the Depression.

1097. Author of *Hurry Home*, he was the second African-American to win a Rhodes Scholarship, in 1963.

1098. Which of Alice Childress' plays won the first Obie Award in 1956 for best original Off-Broadway play?

1099. Ed Bullins was Minister of Culture for this short-lived San Francisco group of black artists and political activists in the 1960's.

1100. This play by Ed Bullins, part of *The Electronic Nigger and Others*, won the Rice Drama Desk Award in 1968.

1101. What important museum of African-American culture is located in Chicago?

1102. Her *Killing Floor*, was the 1978 Lamont Poetry

Selection of the Academy of American Poets.

1103. What black journalist, born in the Civil War, had his poetry collected and published in *Echoes from the Cabin and Elsewhere* in 1905?

SPORTS

Left to Right: Langston Hughes; George Washington Carver; Malcolm X; Frederick Douglass.

SPORTS

1104. He was the first black player in major league baseball.

1105. Elston Howard won the major league Most Valuable Player Award in this year.

1106. De Hart Hubbard was the first black athlete to win this Olympic track and field event in Paris in 1924.

1107. What is Kareem Abdul Jabbar's former name?

1108. Levi Jackson became the first black football captain at this Ivy League college.

1109. Who won the Olympic decathalon in 1960?

1110. He was the first black head coach at the University of Maryland.

1111. Who was the NBA's first black player?

1112. What is football player "Deacon" Jones' real name?

1113. Former Boston Celtic Sam Jones was the first black voted into this state's hall of fame.

1114. Arthur Kennedy, Sr. and Arthur Kennedy, Jr. compete in this sport.

1115. He was the first black college basketball official.

1116. On Oct. 7, 1984 he broke Jim Brown's career rushing record of 12,312 yards.

1117. Who was the first woman to win both the 200 and 400 meter races, setting Olympic and American records in both events?

1118. Jerry Levias was the first black athlete in what athletic conference?

1119. In 1896 he wrote the *Primer of College Football*, the first book of its kind.

1120. Who was the first black tennis player on the Virginia Slims Tour?

1121. This heavyweight champ was nicknamed the "Brown Bomber."

1122. Who was the first black player to pitch a perfect game?

1123. Name the Negro League player nicknamed "Giant Killer" who pitched a perfect, no-hit game.

1124. Pro football great Jim Brown founded this organization.

1125. Joe Brown held a boxing title in this weight class.

1126. Robert S. Brown participated in this daring sport.

1127. Roosevelt "Rosey" Brown was the first black captain of this National Football League team.

1128. He signed a five-year, six million dollar contract with the Houston Oilers, making him the NFL's highest paid player and the league's only starting black quarterback.

1129. Who was major league baseball's first black catcher?

1130. While attending Pasadena Junior College, Jackie Robinson set a new world record for junior college athletes in which track and field event?

1131. With what team in the Negro American League did Jackie Robinson start his professional baseball career?

1132. Boxer Arnold R. Cream adopted this ring name.

1133. In 1982 who became the first pro quarterback to throw for 5,000 yards in a single season?

1134. Who was the first black umpire in major league baseball?

1135. He was the first black U. S. Men's Amateur Tennis champion.

1136. This athlete was the first black U. S. Olympic basketball team member to break into the Amateur Basketball League as well as star on an AAU championship team.

1137. What organization did La Ruth Bostic found?

1138. Wilbert Breland jockeyed in what type of horse racing?

1139. Marlin Briscoe quarterbacked this NFL team.

1140. What was Marlin Briscoe's nickname?

1141. On December 26, 1908 this boxer defeated Tommy Burns to become the first black heavyweight champion.

1142. Whom did Joe Louis knock out on June 22, 1937 to capture the world heavyweight title?

1143. The first major league baseball game in which a black participated was played on this date.

1144. She was the first black woman to win the American Tennis Association (ATP) singles title.

1145. How long did the first black American Tennis Association women's singles champion hold her title, setting a record?

1146. What predominantly white college was first to hire a black physical education instructor?

1147. What black All-American football star at Amherst College and Harvard University was later appointed Assistant Attorney General of the United States in the Taft Administration?

1148. Who was the first black heavyweight boxing champion of America?

1149. What boxer retained the lightweight title from 1901-1908 and was considered by many to have been the "greatest boxer who ever lived?"

1150. What was boxer Henry Armstrong's nickname?

1151. He was the first black sprinter to break into the "world's fastest human" category by co-holding the world's record in the 100 yard dash (9.6 secs.) in 1914.

1152. Who was the first person to broad jump over 25 feet?

1153. He was the first black sprinter to win an Olympic gold medal in the 100 meter dash in 1832.

1154. He won three individual and one team gold medal in the 1936 Olympic Games held in Britain.

1155. In 1904 he became the first black track and field entrant in the modern Olympics.

1156. Whom did Biddle University play in the first black college football game?

1157. What did the C. I. A. A. stand for?

1158. In what year was the first black professional baseball team organized?

1159. The waiters of the Babylon, New York hotel formed this first black professional baseball team.

1160. What was the name of the first black professional baseball team?

1161. This black manager was the first to match black baseball teams against big league clubs in season play.

1162. The black professional baseball pitcher Joe Williams had this nickname.

1163. Richard Hudlin was the first black captain of a varsity sport in what athletic conference?

1164. What university appointed the first black varsity captain in the Big Ten?

1165. This black college, in 1938, organized the first intercollegiate golf championship for blacks.

1166. Who won the first black intercollegiate golf championship?

1167. What tennis champion organized the Philadelphia Tribune Girls Team, a basketball team, in 1931?

1168. In 1946 Jackie Robinson joined the Montreal Royals and lead this league in batting.

1169. In what year, with a batting average of .342, was Jackie Robinson voted the National League's Most Valuable Player?

1170. Whom did Jersey Joe Walcott knock out on July 18, 1951 to win the world heavyweight title?

1171. To whom did Jersey Joe Walcott lose on September 23, 1952 for the heavyweight title?

1172. Where was the 1908 world heavyweight title bout between Jack Johnson and Tommy Burns held?

1173. Who, in 1964, was the first black tennis player to be named to the American Davis Cup squad?

1174. Jesse Owens was the first athlete to surpass this landmark distance in the broad jump.

1175. The first black intercollegiate varsity rower attended this university.

1176. Who was the winner of the first United States Association annual tournament for women?

1177. This black female athlete was a member of six all-collegiate teams during her years at Temple University.

1178. Who was the first black to row intercollegiate varsity crew?

1179. He rode six horses to victory in a single day of racing at Washington Park, Chicago on July 10, 1891.

1180. Who was the first African-American captain of a collegiate track and field team?

1181. He was nominated as the first black captain of a varsity football squad while playing for Amherst College in 1891.

1182. Jackie Robinson left baseball in 1957 to assume a post as vice-president and member of the board of this company.

1183. Who was the first black to captain a collegiate basketball team?

1184. What university in 1908 became the first school to have a black basketball team captain?

1185. What university's team elected the first black collegiate track and field captain?

1186. This was the first association organized to promote and control athletes at black schools.

1187. The record of the most track and field gold medals won by a woman at a single Olympics was set in this city.

1188. In 1960, who won the track and field gold medals in the 100 meter, 200 meter and 4x400 women's relay race?

1189. He won All-Pro and Pro-Bowl Honors 3 years in a row as a NFL defensive back.

1190. What black basketball player founded Athletes for a Better Urban Society?

1191. What is Nigerian born boxer and coach Hogan Bassey's nickname?

1192. While playing for the Brooklyn Dodgers he became

the first African-American pitcher to win a World Series game.

1193. Ben Bluitt, a former Detroit high school coach, became this university's first black head coach.

1194. David P. Bolen, a former Olympic quarter miler, was later appointed U. S. Ambassador to this African nation.

1195. Courtland "Crazy Corky" Booze participates in what sport?

1196. Car Carter, a mountain climber, has a mountain named after him in this state.

1197. Who was the first black athlete to represent the United States in Olympic gymnastics?

1198. Who was the first black athlete to win the Heisman Trophy?

1199. Tyari Casel adopted the nickname "Mr. Kung Fu" through his participation in what sport?

1200. Who was the third black to break major league baseball's "color line?"

1201. The third black major leaguer played centerfield for this team.

1202. "Sweetwater" Clifton played for what famous basketball squad after retiring from the NBA?

1203. What famous pitcher did Bill Drake teach?

1204. The first black Heisman Trophy winner was afflicted with this disease.

1205. This Green Bay Packer went on to become a beer distributor in Los Angeles and an NBC sports analyst.

1206. Who was the American League's first black baseball player?

1207. Who founded and coached the Renaissance basketball team?

1208. Bill "Plunk" Drake pitched for what all-black team?

1209. Walter Dukes, former New York Knicks basketball player, was president and co-founder of this African-American foundation.

1210. Joe Gilliam, Jr. was the NFL's first African-American to play this position.

1211. Everett "Monster Man" Eddy is an expert in this sport.

1212. This is the nickname of the originator of the "Rufus Shuttle."

1213. He was the only black general manager of a major league sports team, the Milwaukee Bucks.

1214. Who in June, 1986 received his bachelor's degree from the University of Massachusetts after having dropped out to play professional basketball?

1215. He was Spain's first American-born black matador.

1216. Richard Ewell and Michelle McCladdie became the first black couple in this professional sports organization.

1217. What professional football player introduced the "Rufus Shuttle?"

1218. Theodore Flowers was the first black boxer to win the championship in which weight class?

1219. What was boxer Theodore Flowers' nickname?

1220. He was the first Bahamian pitcher in the American League.

1221. Andrew "Rube" Foster founded what professional sports league?

1222. Kid Gavilan, former welterweight champion, was a member of this heavyweight champion's training camp.

1223. At what major university was Dennis Franklin the first black quarterback?

1224. What was heavyweight champ Joe Frazier's nickname?

1225. This Pullman porter also played outfield for the Chicago American Giants.

1226. Who was the 1965 Heisman Trophy award winner?

1227. Robert "Pappy" Gault was the first U. S. Olympic coach of what team?

1228. What Cuban-born boxer nicknamed "The Hawk" created the "Bolo Punch?"

1229. What tennis champion and golfer earned her place in the Black Hall of Fame in 1974?

1230. Nicknamed "Cookie" this professional fullback organized the United States Coalition in 1975.

1231. Who was the first black to play with the Washington Senators?

1232. What National League team did Larry Doby coach after his career as a major league baseball player?

1233. What is "Dr. J's" full name?

1234. Who was the Los Angeles Dodger's first black coach?

1235. What was the nickname of the first black NFL quarterback?

1236. Drag racer Nellie Gains is also known by this name.

1237. At what university was Walt Fordon the first black player and coach?

1238. This former boxer owns Motown Industries.

1239. This first black justice in Massachusetts was the first athlete to broad jump over 25 feet.

1240. Who was the fourth African-American to enter organized baseball?

1241. In what year did Archie Griffin win the Heisman Trophy?

1242. George "Rotation Slim" Hairston was a champion of this sport.

1243. Name the record-breaking 1960's jockey from Atlantic City, New Jersey.

1244. Who coached Morehouse's first football team?

1245. Which former Globetrotter was touted as "The World's Best Dribbler," and founded the Harlem Magicians?

1246. What sports historian was elected into the Black Hall of Fame in 1974?

1247. This former longshoreman was President Gerald Ford's high school football teammate.

1248. Who was the first black professional basketball coach in the now defunct American Basketball League?

1249. Who was "The Black Globetrotter" of heavyweight boxing?

1250. Mike Mason was the second African-American athlete to play in this professional sports league.

1251. Willie "Say Hey" Mays was elected into the Black Hall of Fame in what year?

1252. What Olympic track star became Chicago City Commissioner and an Illinois Congressman?

1253. As the coach of the Tennessee State football team, he was voted Coach of the Year in 1972.

1254. Who was the first African-American player traded in major league baseball?

1255. Who was the 1952 light heavyweight boxing champion and founder of the Any Boy Can program?

1256. He was the first black member of the National Association of the NAIA (National Association of Intercollegiate Athletics) Executive Committee.

1257. Who was the first black contestant in a billiards tournament?

1258. What pro football lineman was voted "Guard of the Century" in 1970?

1259. In 1956, at age 21, who became the youngest fighter to win the world heavyweight title?

1260. What Brown University football player was the first black to participate in the Rose Bowl?

1261. He was the first black major league baseball ✓ manager.

1262. What black boxing champion did John W. Roxborough discover and manage?

1263. Who was the first African-American coach in a professional sports league?

1264. In 1966, they became the first professional athletic team to appoint a black coach.

1265. As the first American black boxer to receive recognition, he is referred to in the *Life and Journals of Lord Byron*.

1266. Who, in 1940, fought Buddy Baer at a benefit for the Navy Emergency Relief Department?

1267. This former baseball pitcher became president, general manager and field manager of the Chicago American Giants.

1268. Frank Grant first invented this indispensable piece of baseball equipment.

1269. What light heavyweight boxing champion was nicknamed "The Magnificent Mongoose"?

1270. What university planted the oak trees won by Jesse Owens at the Berlin Olympic games?

1271. After the first black baseball team was organized in 1885, what name was attached to nearly every all-black team for 25 years?

1272. In 1879, this black jockey won 35 of the 75 races he entered, including the Travers Stakes at Saratoga.

1273. The first significant black-white boxing match ended in a draw in which round?

1274. Called the "Colored King," he won the bicycle racing sprint championship of America.

1275. What 1908 collegiate 400-yard dash champion won the 1600 meter relay at the Olympic Games in London?

1276. What legendary figure in black tennis owned her own tennis courts in Chicago where she taught the game to young African-Americans?

1277. With what team did Wilt Chamberlain begin his National Basketball Association career?

1278. What African-American football end was named to Walter Camp's All-American team in 1917?

1279. In 1925 the Boston Athletic Club refused admission to a football player from this university on the grounds that he was black.

1280. In what year were the Harlem Globetrotters organized?

1281. Who led the United States Olympic basketball team to the gold medal in 1956?

1282. Wilt Chamberlain left college to play with this professional basketball team.

1283. What year did Jackie Robinson lead UCLA's football team to an undefeated season and lead the Pacific Coast basketball conference in scoring?

1284. This pitcher led his team to a Negro League World Series for the second time in 1946 after pitching 64 consecutive scoreless innings during the season.

1285. Who was the welterweight boxing champion from

1946 through 1951?

1286. In what year were nearly one half of all the boxers listed in *Ring Magazine* black?

1287. How long did Joe Louis retain the world heavyweight boxing championship before he retired in 1949?

1288. What team signed the first black player in the National Basketball Association?

1289. Who was the first black to be accepted to compete in the National Tennis Championship at Forest Hills, New York?

1290. Who was the light heavyweight boxing champion from 1952 to 1961?

1291. This New York Giant won the National League batting title and the Most Valuable Player award in 1954.

1292. Who was the first black member of the Professional Golfers Association?

1293. From 1957 to his retirement in 1966, this All-League fullback broke every rushing record in the NFL.

1294. He was NBA scoring champion for seven years in a row, from 1959 to 1965.

1295. In 1968, he became the No. 1 American tennis player after winning the National Open and the Men's Singles championship at Forest Hills, New York.

1296. Who proposed a black boycott of the 1968 Olympic games?

1297. Thomas E. "Satch" Sanders coached basketball at this Ivy League college.

1298. Who was the first black golfer to win a major tournament?

1299. In 1969, this major golf tournament became the first won by an African-American.

1300. A two-time Kentucky Derby winner, he was the first American to win the English Sweepstakes.

1301. Who was the World Tennis Team's first black player?

1302. Chicago's first black judge, Fred Wayman "Duke" Slater, played pro football for this team.

1303. She was the first black woman to hold a first degree black belt in judo.

1304. What major league baseball player won the Springarn Medal in 1975?

1305. Who was the first black female member of the Amateur Fencers League?

1306. Who was the only baseball player to play in all four Negro World Series?

1307. Abe Saperstein organized this performing black professional basketball team.

1308. Althea Gibson and this woman won the doubles championship at Wimbledon in 1951.

1309. What is Harlem Globetrotters Reese Tatum Sr.'s nickname?

1310. He was the first black trainer for harness racing horses.

1311. Cincinati Reds infielder Bobby Tolan was the first

black recipient of this award.

1312. Who was the first black National Football League head coach?

1313. He was the first black professional major league hockey player.

1314. Who was the first black female jockey, winning for the first time on September 2, 1971?

1315. This fencer was the youngest winner of the National Women's Foil Championship.

1316. Who is the only American sprinter to have been named to five Olympic teams?

1317. Track star Malvin Greston Whitfield was the first black winner of this award.

1318. He was the first black umpire in the National League.

1319. Maurice Morning "Maury" Wills was voted Professional Athlete of the Year in what year?

1320. Who was the first African-American´ to win the National Public Links Golf Tournament?

1321. NFL player Paul "Tank" Younger was the first black inducted into this state's Hall of Fame.

1322. Willie Oliver, Andy Washington, Al Pullins, Byron Lang and Walter Wright were the original members of what all-black team?

1323. In 1965 this Chicago Bears rookie scored six touchdowns in one game and 22 overall.

1324. Who was the first African-American official in the

National Football League?

1325. After winning the 1965 Heisman Trophy, he received a $350,000 salary and bonus to play for the Kansas City Chiefs.

1326. Which Boston Celtic star in 1966 owned a 1,500-acre rubber plantation in Liberia and a restaurant in Boston?

1327. Which Negro League pitcher published his autobiography in 1963 titled *Maybe I'll Pitch Forever*?

1328. When was the first black-sponsored float entered in the annual Pasadena, California Rose Bowl Parade?

1329. He became the 24th world heavyweight champion with his 7th round technical knockout of Sonny Liston in Miami, Florida in 1964.

1330. What is "Sonny" Liston's real name?

1331. What team did Oscar Robertson play for in 1964 when he was the only player unanimously voted to the NBA's All-Star Team?

1332. Who was the second black to win a Pro Golfers Association-sponsored tournament?

1333. He passed up 115 offers from various colleges and committed himself to attending the University of Louisville in May, 1964.

1334. He won a total of three gold medals in the 1948 and 1952 Olympics, and in 1964 was appointed U. S. Information Agency Youth Officer in Kenya.

1335. Whose appointment as U. S. women's Olympic track coach in 1960 and 1964 resulted in an amendment of the rule barring an Olympic coach from succeeding himself?

1336. In 1964, what school's entire 440 relay team won NCAA All-American track and field honors?

1337. Named to a Los Angeles Dodgers coaching position in 1964, he became the fourth African-American to hold a major league coaching position.

1338. When were black baseball players first named Rookie of the Year in both the American and National leagues?

1339. In December 1964 this Boston Celtic scored the 10,000th point of his nine-year pro basketball career.

1340. Who was the first American to reach the last round of the World Junior Fencing Championship?

1341. What is Muhammad Ali's former name?

1342. Emlen Tunnell was this NFL team's first black player.

1343. In 1965 who signed a $70,000 contract with the New York Yankees to become the highest paid athlete in the history of professional baseball?

1344. Selected captain of the 1965-66 basketball team, he became the first black captain of a varsity sport at the University of Minnesota.

1345. He was the first University of Michigan athlete to receive the Big Ten conference's most valuable player award.

1346. What school first named a black to a varsity coaching spot in the Big Ten conference?

1347. He participated in the fastest heavyweight bout in history by knocking out Sonny Liston in the first minute of the first round.

1348. Charles Price was hired in May 1965 as head football coach of the predominately white Langley High School, the first black in this state at such a position.

1349. Who played his 1,400th baseball game for the Cincinnati Reds in June, 1965 to set a team record?

1350. Who was the first black to be named to a Big Ten varsity coaching post?

1351. What was the name of the first African-American professional baseball team to tour the country?

1352. In 1875 Oscar Lewis became the first black to win the Kentucky Derby, riding this horse to victory.

1353. This player became the first black to play professional football for a major team in 1919.

1354. With what team did Fritz Pollard start his pro football career?

1355. When was the first black post season "bowl" game played between Atlanta University and Prairie View University?

1356. Roy Campanella became the first African-American to manage an organized baseball team on the field while he caught for Nashua, New Hampshire in this league.

1357. Who was the first black pitcher in the major leagues?

1358. When did the first black pitcher enter major league baseball?

1359. What was the first black post season "bowl" football game?

1360. He was the first African-American to win baseball's MVP three times, in 1951, 1953, and 1955.

1361. The first black in organized hockey played for what team?

1362. He was the first athlete to high jump over 7 feet.

1363. He was the first African-American to coach an integrated pro basketball team.

1364. What was the first integrated pro basketball team to be coached by a black?

1365. In the 1971 World Series, he became the second player in history to hit safely in every series game.

1366. Who was the first National Basketball Association player to score 30,000 career points?

1367. Who was the first black, in 1950, to play organized hockey?

1368. Bob Douglas was the first African-American to be elected to the basketball Hall of Fame, after owning and coaching what fabled all-black team?

1369. What was the nickname of the Harlem Renaissance Five basketball team?

1370. The first African-American to win 200 football games coached at this university.

1371. After 31 pro victories, Muhammad Ali lost his first fight to whom?

1372. This welterweight champion fought under the name Melody Jackson.

1373. What team signed major league baseball's first black pitcher?

1374. Who was the first African-American football coach to win 200 games?

1375. He was Georgia Tech's first quarterback and set 13 team records.

1376. Who was the first black to pitch in the American League?

1377. Who was the black professional playing for a Newcastle, Pennsylvania team in 1822?

1378. In the early 1900's, this New York Giants manager tried to bring black players to his team by representing them as American Indians.

1379. The all-black Harlem Globetrotters originally played under this name in the 1920s.

1380. Signed to a 10-year, $22 million contract in 1981, be became baseball's highest paid player.

1381. Who was the eighth black Heisman Trophy winner in 1981 while at University of Southern California?

1382. In what year did a black first pitch in the American League?

1383. In what league was the first integrated pro basketball team to be coached by a black?

1384. Lee Elder was the first African-American golfer to qualify for this tournament.

1385. Who is acknowledged by many to be the greatest offensive back in football's history?

1386. Who was the first rookie to be named Most Valuable Player of the National Basketball Association All-Star game?

1387. After dropping out of college after his junior year, Julius Erving signed a $500,000 contract over four years with what American Basketball Association team?

1388. Who was the first African-American golfer to reach $1 million in career earnings?

1389. Who holds the record of 100 points scored in a single NBA game?

1390. The Harlem Globetrotters played before the largest ever basketball audience of 75,000 fans in what stadium?

1391. He began as a basketball player with the Harlem Globetrotters, but went on to become one of baseball's greatest pitchers with the St. Louis Cardinals.

1392. He became the first black athlete to win an intercollegiate weight championship when he threw the hammer 162 feet, four and one-half inches in 1912.

1393. Who was the first African-American to play at Wimbledon?

1394. He is known as "Mr. October."

1395. Joe DiMaggio called him "the best pitcher I ever faced."

1396. Who was the Associated Press U. S. Female Athlete of the Year and United Press International's Athlete of the Year in 1960?

1397. Bill Russell led this college to two consecutive NCAA titles and 60 consecutive wins.

1398. After he graduated from the University of Southern California and won football's Heisman Trophy in 1968, he set a world record in the 440 yard dash, and was voted

College Player of the Decade.

1399. After helping the Miami Dolphins win three consecutive Super Bowls, Paul Warfield signed a seven-figure contract in 1975 with what World Football League team?

1400. When was the first world series between Negro League teams played?

1401. In 1920 this, the first African-American league was formed.

1402. Walter Payton gained 275 yards in 1977, for a single game record against this team.

1403. Hank Aaron began his baseball career with this black team.

1404. Who holds the all-time career home run record?

1405. Who was the "Babe Ruth of Negro Baseball"?

1406. In 1977 he broke Ty Cobb's 1928 record of 892 stolen bases.

1407. What is Walter Payton's nickname?

1408. At quarterback, Warren Moon led this Canadian Football League team to five straight championships.

1409. Who was the NFL's first regular starting quarterback?

1410. She won a gold medal in the 1984 L. A. Olympics for her record-setting performance in the 200 meter run.

1411. In 1982 he signed a $13.2 million, 6-year contract with the Philadelphia 76ers to become sport's highest-paid team athlete for a single season.

1412. He became the Professional Rodeo Cowboys Association's first black champion in 1983.

1413. When did a black first qualify for the Masters Golf Tournament?

1414. Who is the only pitcher credited with two World Series home runs?

1415. Satchel Paige got his nickname because this part of his body was "satchel-sized."

1416. The first black Chicago Cub, he was the first slugger to use a light bat.

1417. Arthur Dumas high-jumped a record seven feet in 1956 while a freshman at this college.

1418. She was the country's first black woman sports car racer.

1419. Who was the second black player to be elected to the Baseball Hall of Fame?

1420. What African-American hurdler participated in the 1904 Olympic Games?

1421. Who was the first black player in the American Baseball League?

1422. She was the first African-American professional ice skater.

1423. A catcher, he was the first black to play for the New York Yankees baseball team.

1424. This African-American jockey won the very first Kentucky Derby.

1425. Who was major league baseball's first black coach?

1426. Who was the first African-American major league hockey star?

1427. He won the Kentucky Derby in 1901 and 1902.

1428. For what baseball team did the first black in the American League play?

1429. Who is the only jockey to have ridden three winners in the Kentucky Derby?

1430. This athlete was the National Football League's rushing leader from 1957-1965

1431. What boxer won the 1960 Olympic gold medal?

1432. A gold medalist in the 1968 200-meter dash, he wore a black glove, black socks, and a black scarf to protest African-American inequality.

1433. What heavyweight boxer marched around the ring with the American flag after winning the gold medal in the 1968 Olympics?

1434. A bronze medalist in the 200-meter dash in the 1968 Olympics, he raised a gloved hand at the victory ceremony.

1435. What was the name of the horse ridden by Isaac Murphy in his first Kentucky Derby in 1884?

1436. A Winston-Salem State University basketball coach, his victories rank him among the top four in history.

1437. Who ended Joe Louis' career by knocking him out in Madison Square Garden in 1951?

1438. In what year did the first African-Americans become members of the National Basketball Association?

1439. Who was the first black professional football player in 1946?

1440. What running back became the first African-American to play for the University of Alabama?

1441. For what team did the first black pro football player run?

1442. Who established the professional baseball record of 130 stolen bases?

1443. When did the first black play for Paul (Bear) Bryant at the University of Alabama?

1444. What player integrated the New York Giants in 1949?

1445. Who was the first player to be drafted out of high school in National Basketball Association history?

1446. What player, stricken by encephalitis, received financial assistance through a benefit game of pro basketball stars?

1447. Name the important summer basketball league attracting pro and college stars in Philadelphia.

1448. In what year did the National Association of Baseball issue a statement denying admission to any team with a black player?

1449. What college did Jesse Owens attend?

1450. In 1962, he became the first black player to enter the Baseball Hall of Fame.

1451. A pitcher in the Negro Baseball League for 25 years, developer of the bat-badger, jumpball and drooper, he was elected to the Baseball Hall of Fame in 1971.

1452. Who threw the pitch that Hank Aaron hit for his 715th career home run, breaking Babe Ruth's record?

1453. For what team in the Negro leagues did Satchel Paige play?

1454. What player received the distinction of being named Most Valuable Player in both baseball leagues?

1455. What was the Supreme Court vote on Muhammad Ali's draft-evasion case when overturned in 1971?

1456. In what city did Muhammad Ali defeat his opponent in 1974 to regain his title for the then richest bout in history?

1457. What American league baseball team appointed the first black manager in the sport's history in 1974?

1458. Whom did Muhammad Ali defeat to regain his heavy-weight boxing crown in 1974?

1459. In what year did Muhammad Ali refuse induction into the Armed Forces?

1460. Name the African-American who was the first director of physical education for Harvard University.

1461. Not recruited by Coach Bud Wilkinson, he earned an athletic scholarship and became the first black on Oklahoma University's football team.

1462. Whites attacked African-Americans throughout the country after Jack Johnson defeated what heavyweight challenger at Reno on July 4, 1910?

1463. Who organized the first paid black baseball team composed of waiters and bellhops in 1885?

1464. To whom did Jack Johnson lost his heavyweight title to in Cuba, 1915?

1465. A halfback at Brown University, he was named an All-American in 1916.

1466. Who became the first black captain of a predominately white football team at Massachusetts State in 1905?

1467. Who was the abstaining justice in the Supreme Court's overturning of Muhammad Ali's draft evasion case in 1974?

1468. A home-run hitting shortstop, he became the first National League player to win the Most Valuable Player award two years in succession.

1469. This renowned baseball catcher became paralyzed after a 1958 automobile accident.

1470. Who was the unsuccessful challenger of baseball's reserve clause in a 1972 Supreme Court decision?

1471. What catcher reportedly hit 80 home runs in one season for the Homestead Grays?

1472. He broke Babe Ruth's record of World Series home runs in 1977.

1473. A pitcher for the Brooklyn Dodgers, he won 20 games in his rookie year.

1474. How many lifetime homeruns did Willie Mays hit?

1475. This undefeated girls basketball club prospered in the 1940's.

1476. What Los Angeles Laker scored 71 points against the

New York Knickerbockers?

1477. In 1968, he was named College Basketball Player of the Year over Lew Alcindor.

1478. He was the first black scout for the National Basketball Association.

1479. What is Oscar Robertson's nickname.

1480. How many games did the University of Cincinnati lose when Oscar Robertson played for them?

1481. Rated the greatest bantamweight of all time, he was a champion for 11 years.

1482. To whom did Joe Gans lose his title in 1908?

1483. Considered the greatest welterweight of all time, he was the oldest to win the heavyweight crown.

1484. What was Sugar Ray Robinson's real name?

1485. To whom did Muhammad Ali lose his title in 1978?

1486. He knocked out more opponents than any other man in boxing.

1487. Who was the only boxer to hold the championship in three divisions at once?

1488. Who was the dominant featherweight champion during the 1950's?

1489. What well-known, black-sponsored, post-season football bowl game is dominated by Florida A&M University?

1490. What black man was the first American to fight for the heavyweight championship of the world against Tom

Crib in 1810?

1491. Name the featherweight boxer who fought a 70-round draw.

1492. Louisiana lightweight Andy Bowen fought the longest boxing contest in history, lasting how many rounds?

1493. Name the lightweight champion in 1943 whose real name was Sidney Walker.

1494. This jockey won the first running of the Futurity in 1888.

1495. In the first Kentucky Derby running in 1875, how many of the 15 jockeys were black?

1496. Who was the first American jockey to shorten his stirrup in the famed crouch position?

1497. Name the black bicycle club formed in 1892 in New York City.

1498. This black baseball team was considered the best in the South in 1910.

1499. For whom was Willie Mays playing when drafted by the New York Giants?

1500. Who quarterbacked the Washington and Jefferson team in the 1922 Rose Bowl?

1501. This two-time All-American from Syracuse University died of leukemia in 1963.

1502. A clever boxer, nicknamed "Boston Tar Baby," he knocked down Jack Johnson in 1906.

1503. How many cities had black-owned golf clubs in 1928?

1504. Who was the first black to gain admission to the U.S. Lawn Tennis Men's Singles Championship?

1505. She won the Women's Singles Championship at Wimbledon, England in 1957.

1506. He held the AAU Championship in the 200-yard dash for 1912 and 1913.

1507. Who was the first black Olympian?

1508. In 1916, he equaled the world record in the 440-yard dash while at the University of Chicago.

1509. She was the first woman to win three Olympic gold medals.

1510. What is the name of the Tennessee State University's women's relay teams?

1511. He was the first black to play basketball for the University of Houston.

1512. How old was Jersey Joe Walcott when he won the heavyweight boxing championship in 1951?

1513. How many rounds did the first fight between African-American Tom Molineaux and Tom Crib last?

1514. This champion cyclist invented a steel bicycle rim.

1515. In what year did Ralph Metcalfe run in the Olympics?

1516. What two black athletes were thrown out of the Olympic village during the 1968 Olympics for "defiance and militancy"?

1517. In what year were the first blacks inducted in baseball's Hall of Fame?

1518. He won the Kentucky Derby twice, had a picaresque riding career in Russia and Europe, and died in Paris.

ENTERTAINMENT

Above (l. to r.): Louis Armstrong; Mahalia Jackson; Scott Joplin.

ENTERTAINMENT

1519. Nicknamed "Leadbelly," this one-time inmate of Louisiana's notorious Angola penitentiary sang and composed work songs.

1520. This New Orleans jazz pianist, Ferdinand Joseph la Menthe Morton, won international fame under what nickname?

1521. The subject of a popular blues song, this street in the red-light district of New Orleans is commonly thought of as the birth of jazz.

1522. What coronet player performed for all-white audiences in New Orleans bordellos and died in a Louisiana state mental hospital?

1523. Credited with having popularized gospel music as a modern art form, she first attracted national attention through her association with Martin Luther King Jr.

1524. Released in 1920, "Crazy Blues" established this singer as the first commercially successful blues vocalist.

1525. This form of popular entertainment, featuring Mr. Tam and Mr. Bones, was popular between 1845 and 1900.

1526. What lame stablehand from Louisville served as inspiration for a blackface character created by Thomas Dartmouth Rice in the 1820's?

1527. This individual's dancing was compared by Charles Dickens in *American Notes* (1842) to "fingers on a tambourine."

1528. Name the composer of "Carry Me Back to Ole Virginny" and "Oh Dem Golden Slippers."

1529. What play, once the most frequently performed work on the American stage, was often burlesqued in post-bellum minstrel shows?

1530. This ragtime composer wrote the opera, *Treemonisha,* which was performed only once, in 1915.

1531. Sales of this famous blues singer's recordings were rumored to have kept the Columbia Company from bankruptcy during the early twenties.

1532. He is credited with establishing a "boogie woogie" bass line which is still used frequently.

1533. Duke Ellington first won recognition playing at this Harlem nightclub.

1534. What pianist's 1939 appearance with the Benny Goodman Orchestra marked the beginning of the desegregation of jazz music?

1535 A master of the be-bob idiom, this trumpet player in 1963 petitioned the California Secretary of State to be included as an independent candidate for President of the United States.

1536. After a leg injury ended his professional boxing aspirations, this soul singer formed a music group known as the Famous Flames.

1537. Originally prominent as a pianist, this pop singer also portrayed W.C. Handy in the film, *St. Louis Blues.*

1538. Considered by many to be the greatest jazz trumpeter since Louis Armstrong, he has also been instrumental in influencing the styles of Herbie Hancock and John Coltrane.

1539. In May, 1965, the Pulitzer Prize Advisory Board voted against honoring this bandleader, composer, and pianist.

1540. "Amateur Night" at this Harlem theatre launched the careers of both Ella Fitzgerald and Billie Holiday.

1541. Since the release of her first hit, "A-tisket, A-tasket," in 1938, this singer has won unprecedented acclaim.

1542. This bandleader has composed numerous motion picture scores and has served as musical director and arranger for Peggy Lee, Frank Sinatra and Sarah Vaughan.

1543. Harlem's main "jump joint" during the 1920's, this segregated club was famous for its singing and dancing black waiters.

1544. A distinctly Harlem entertainment, this type of gathering served as an alternative to segregated nightclubs for Harlem residents.

1545. His Georgia Minstrels were the first successful all-black theatrical troupe.

1546. This theatrical team became famous for popularizing the cakewalk at the turn of the century.

1547. Billed as "The Minstrel King," this popular entertainer claimed to have "the largest mouth in the world."

1548. Dan Emmet's play, *Dixie,* was first performed on April 4, 1859, in what city?

1549. This 1902 musical comedy, starring Bert Williams and George Walker, was the first successful black production which deviated from the minstrel format.

1550. Organized in 1914, this Harlem company staged all-black performances of such plays as *Dr. Jekyll and Mr. Hyde* and *The Count of Monte Cristo.*

1551. This 1921 show featured music by Eubie Blake and Noble Sissle, including, "I'm Just Wild About Harry."

1552. Flournoy Miller and Aubrey Lyle's musical, *Runnin' Wild,* created a sensation when it opened in 1924 by introducing what popular dance?

1553. His score for the 1929 musical, *Hot Chocolates,* included the hit, "Ain't Misbehavin'."

1554. W.E.B. DuBois supported what short-lived Harlem theatrical troupe?

1555. Three of his plays -- *The Rider of Dreams, Granny Maumee,* and *Simon the Cyrenian* -- were staged at Broadway's Garden Theatre in 1917.

1556. This actor created the title role of Eugene O'Neill's *The Emperor Jones,* in 1921.

1557. Although she first won acclaim as a jazz singer, she is best remembered for her films, including *The Sound and the Fury, Pinky,* and *The Member of the Wedding.*

1558. Nicknamed "Satchmo," this jazz trumpeter has appeared in over 35 motion pictures.

1559. In 1974, this jazz pianist and composer recorded an

album live at the Montreux Jazz Festival, entitled, *91 Years Young.*

1560. Born in Pittsburgh in 1914, he became the first African-American pop idol, often scoring with such hits as "Tenderly," "I Apologize," and "No One But You."

1561. This great jazz vocalist died in July, 1959, while being detained for drug possession.

1562. Mentor to Bessie Smith and known as the "Mother of the Blues," Gertrude Malissa Pridgett became famous under what name?

1563. Born in New York in 1925, this jazz drummer first drew attention through his association with Charlie Parker in the late 1940's.

1564. Born Ruth Jones in Tuscaloosa, Alabama, she was later nicknamed "The Queen."

1565. On hearing the music made by his slaves, Thomas Jefferson observed that this instrument, brought from Africa, was proper to them.

1566. This dance, popular along the Mississippi River during the 1800's, simulated the handling of freight on steamboats.

1567. In 1757, James Fenimore Cooper described this New York holiday as filled with songs and energetic dances of African origin.

1568. Constructed of bamboo joints, this small drum gave its proper name to a dance in New Orleans during the 1800's.

1569. According to *Paxton's Directory of 1822,* New Orleans blacks congregated on this famous square to "dance, carouse, and debauch on the Sabbath."

1570. The main feature of this dance popular during the 1850's was the movement of the heels and toes without changing the position of the legs, so that performers appeared to glide across the floor.

1571. One time a member of the Spinners, he was a superb producer, songwriter and singer for Motown.

1572. Gaudily dressed and smart-talking, this stereotypical minstrel character served as a foil for Jim Crow.

1573. This British King took banjo lessons from James Bohee, an African-American minstrel whose company toured Europe after the Civil War.

1574. This actor, known as "the Grand Old Man of the Negro Theatre," appeared in the first all-black version of *Uncle Tom's Cabin.*

1575. In what year was the first filmed version of *Uncle Tom's Cabin* produced?

1576. In 1891, at the age of 12, this future dancing star made his debut in a stage musical, *The South Before the War.*

1577. This 1889 all-black musical was the first New York production to omit blackface makeup and include black women in its chorus.

1578. This popular dance was the first appearance of a black movement to be assimilated into white ballroom dancing.

1579. This 1898 musical was the first show to be organized, produced, and managed by African-Americans.

1580. This celebrated poet wrote lyrics for the early black musical *Clorindy -- The Origin of the Cakewalk.*

1581. W. C. Fields called this black minstrel player "the funniest man I ever saw and the saddest man I ever knew."

1582. This famous Voodoo priestess of New Orleans is credited with initiating the St. John's Eve Celebrations on Lake Pontchartrain.

1583. Produced in Harlem's Lafayette Theatre in 1913, this musical revue was the first black entertainment to attract large white audiences.

1584. Name the circuit of black vaudeville performers.

1585. Known as "little Blackbird," this popular musical comedy star debuted with Josephine Baker in Blake and Sissle's *Shuffle Along.*

1586. Her film credits include *Broadway Rhythm, Cabin in the Sky, Till Clouds Roll By,* and *The Wiz.*

1587. Hailed by Europeans as the embodiment of "le jazz hot," this American dancer became a star after appearing at the Folies Bergeres in Paris in 1926.

1588. In 1933, he became the first black dancer to perform at New York's Metropolitan Opera Company.

1589. He played the street singer in the 1964 European film of Brecht's *Three Penny Opera,* and sang the hit song, "Mac the Knife."

1590. This all-black Virginia college became, during the 1920's, a center for dance based on African heritage.

1591. The NAACP tried to stop the filming of what 1947 Disney movie because of the stereotyped character of Uncle Remus?

1592. In what year did the first formal black ballet troupe debut in New York?

1593. In 1934, his production *Kykunkor* was the first commercially successful dance production to incorporate African rhythms, costumes, songs, and steps.

1594. A scholar of West Indian dance and culture, she also originated the role of Georgia Browne in the 1946 Broadway musical, *Cabin in the Sky*.

1595. After beginning her dance career in New York's "Cafe Society," she studied slave dancing in the American South and was named director of Liberia's Performing Arts Center in 1959.

1596. Born in Texas in 1931, he appeared in numerous Broadway musicals during the 1950's, and in 1958 formed the American Dance Theatre.

1597. Ava Gardner won the role of Julie the mulatto over Lena Horne in this MGM musical of 1951.

1598. Premiere *danseuse* of the Metropolitan Opera Ballet from 1951 to 1954, she was the first American black ballerina.

1599. This 1954 all-black musical marked the New York debut of Alvin Ailey, Arthur Mitchell, and Carmen de Lavallade.

1600. The first black ballet dancer with the New York City Ballet, he founded the Dance Theatre of Harlem in 1970.

1601. Born in Trinidad, he has become prominent as a dancer, choreographer, photographer, singer, writer, costume designer, and proponent of the "Un-Cola."

1602. In this year, delegates of the NAACP met for the first time with Hollywood executives to discuss pejorative racial roles and the desegregation of studio labor.

1603. In this year, *Uncle Tom's Cabin* was produced by the Thomas Edison Company and starred a white man, Edwin S. Porter, in blackface.

1604. This film, originally entitled *The Clansman*, inspired a nationwide boycott by the NAACP in 1915.

1605. This black-produced and directed film which opened in 1918 was intended as a response to Griffith's *The Birth of a Nation*.

1606. This mailman from Omaha founded the Lincoln Motion Picture Company in 1916, the first black-financed production company in Los Angeles.

1607. In 1939, this actress won the first Oscar ever given to a black performer.

1608. This silent film star was known during the 1920's as "the black Valentino."

1609. A popular nightclub performer, he has appeared in the films *Sweet Charity*, *The Three Penny Opera*, *Young Man with a Horn*, *The Benny Goodman Story*, and *Rufus Jones for President*.

1610. Peggy Pettit, Leslie Uggams, and Ruby Dee appeared in this 1973 filmed drama concerning three generations of black women.

1611. Often criticized for playing stereotypical subservient roles, this actor appeared in over 40 films between 1930 and 1974.

1612. His Academy Award was earned by his portrayal of a tough-talking military man in *An Officer and a Gentleman*.

1613. Among his many film roles is that of Lieutenant Lothar Zogg, an Air Force bombadier in, *Dr. Strangelove or:*

How I Learned to Stop Worrying and Love the Bomb.

1614. This actor appeared in several of Frank Capra's films during the 1930's, and in 1975 played an octogenarian shoeshine man in *Car Wash.*

1615. Brock Peters played Tom Robinson, wrongfully arrested for raping a white girl in this film based on Harper Lee's novel.

1616. In this 1950 Fox release, Sidney Poitier plays a doctor who unjustly becomes the object of a town's hatred and scorn.

1617. He became famous playing John Shaft, the Harlem private eye, during the early 1970's.

1618. Although she appeared in a supporting role in *Guess Who's Coming to Dinner,* she is best known as television's Louise Jefferson.

1619. Cicely Tyson plays Portia, an articulate and militant maid in this 1968 screen adaptation of a Carson McCuller novel.

1620. Paired with Diana Ross in *Lady Sings the Blues* and *Mahogany,* he also played Scott Joplin in a 1977 fictionalized film biography.

1621. As well as having acted in over 40 feature films, Sidney Poitier has also received screen writing credit for this 1968 production.

1622. This jazz trumpeter wrote dialogue and music for *The Hat,* a cartoon which depicts the origins of international conflict.

1623. This Motown producer's first screen undertaking was *Mahogany,* which he directed.

1624. Known primarily as an actress, she received screen writing credits for *Up Tight*, a film examining the black power movement after King's death and based loosely on Liam O'Flaherty's novel, *The Informer*.

1625. Butterfly McQueen plays a maid who cries at the slightest provocation in this 1941 comedy starring Rita Hayworth and Merle Oberon.

1626. He played Buckwheat in countless "Our Gang" episodes during the 1930's.

1627. She plays a Bessie Smith-style blues singer in *All the Fine Young Cannibals*, the story of a white musician's career in the jazz world.

1628. This 1974 United Artist release has Moms Mabley leading the campaign of a black candidate for mayor of Baltimore.

1629. This celebrated composer and bandleader appeared as Pie Eye in Otto Preminger's *Anatomy of a Murder*.

1630. Allen Hoskins played this character in numerous films with the "Our Gang" cast.

1631. Cicely Tyson starred in this 1974 television movie, which won nine Emmys, about the fictional life of a 110-year old woman.

1632. This 1958 film featured acts from the Harlem Variety Revue at the Apollo Theatre.

1633. Roscoe Lee Brown plays Babo, who leads the mutiny in this 1965 film adaptation of a Melville novel.

1634. He was famous for his "Minnie the Moocher" and performed it in 1932's *The Big Broadcast*.

1635. His first appearance was in the 1929 *Black and Tan*, where he played his "Black and Tan Fantasy."

1636. He narrated *Body and Soul: Soul, Part II*, a 1968 CBS-TV documentary of soul music in America.

1637. He played "Daddy Rich" in the 1976 movie, *Car Wash*.

1638 This Otto Preminger 1954 film adaptation of Bizet's opera stars Harry Belafonte and pianist Dorothy Dandridge.

1639. He was Sam, who played again "As Time Goes By," in the Bogart-Bergman 1942 classic, *Casablanca*.

1640. Tamara Dobson played the title role in this 1973 film of an international narcotics agent who rids drugs from the black community with good looks, karate, and aid from the community.

1641. This film tells the story of a Caribbean dictatorship though it was filmed in Africa, and starred James Earl Jones, Raymond St. Jacques and Cicely Tyson.

1642. Name Louise Beaver's character in the 1943 MGM effort, *Dubarry was a Lady*, with Red Skelton and Lucille Ball.

1643. Who is the author of *Dutchman*, about a man taunted and abused by a young white female passenger in a New York subway train?

1644. When he produced the film, *Florida Crackers*, this pioneer filmmaker included a graphic lynching scene which was a source of great controversy.

1645. At age 76, this former slave and eminent scientist narrated a 1940 documentary dramatizing his struggles and successes to a young boy pondering the options for the future.

1646. He played himself in *The Greatest*, a 1977 film tracking this man's life from a small-town childhood, through the influence of Malcolm X, to his acceptance of the Muslim faith.

1647. In *A Hero Ain't Nothin' but a Sandwich*, produced in 1977, these two performers play a mother and her live-in companion residing in Watts.

1648. Brian DePalma's 1970 film about life in the 1960's, *Hi Mom*, stars Robert DeNiro and this all-black troupe that performs in white face and blackens the faces of the audiences during the performance.

1649. Paul Winfield, Rex Ingram, Clarence Muse, silent actor George Reed, and even boxing champion Archie Moore have all played this role in various film versions of *The Adventures of Huckleberry Finn*.

1650. Besides roles in *El Condor*, *Dirty Dozen*, and *Kenner*, Jim Brown also played an overzealous marine captain in this 1968 film with Rock Hudson and Patrick McGoohan.

1651. In the 1934 film version of *Imitation of Life*, about a light-skinned black girl who tries to pass for white, what black actress plays the girl's role?

1652. Before becoming a solo singer, he was the lead for the Temptations until 1968.

1653. They played Roy Campanella and his wife in *It's Good to be Alive*, a movie about the baseball great and his tragic, crippling car accident.

1654. He performed with Shirley Temple in the 1938 film, *Just Around the Corner*.

1655. There is a short dramatization of *Uncle Tom's Cabin* in this 1956 Fox musical.

1656. This former pro-footballer was later seen on TV commercials running through airports.

1657. This acclaimed singer made her film debut in the 1972 feature about blues great, Billie Holiday.

1658. He starred with Jack Nicholson in *The Last Detail*, a 1973 movie about two navy servicemen who introduce a young sailor to a "good time" and raise him to maturity.

1659. This jazz vocalist plays a night club singer hooked on drugs in the 1960 feature, *Let No Man Write My Epitaph*.

1660. Canada Lee plays Joe, a steward who saves a drowning woman and child in this Hitchcock classic.

1661. In this 1936 film, the Civil War is on and Shirley Temple and Bill Robinson are Confederate folk who tapdance for train fare to see President Lincoln, hoping he can free her father from a Union prison camp.

1662. Brock Peters, Melba Moore, and Raymond St. Jacques performed in this musical film version of Alan Paton's *Cry, the Beloved Country*.

1663. In the irreverent 1970 movie, *M*A*S*H** Fred Williamson plays an army doctor whose accomplished passing on the football field earned him this nickname.

1664. Diana Ross received an Oscar nomination for costume design for this 1975 movie.

1665. Sammy Davis Jr., Louis Armstrong, and Ossie Davis made this film in 1966, exploring the world and the inner struggles of the black jazz musician.

1666. In *Man Friday*, based on Defoe's classic, *Robinson Crusoe*, this actor actually becomes the master.

1667. Boxer Ken Norton appeared in this 1970 film which paints a particularly violent view of slavery.

1668. This 1968 cult film is one of the few horror films to have a black hero, a young salesman who takes charge of the survivors.

1669. She played the title role in the all-black Broadway version of *Hello Dolly*.

1670. She presented *Your Arms too Short to Box With God* on Broadway in the mid-1970's.

1671. This 1981 Broadway musical focuses on the trials and tribulations of a female trio who must "cross over" to the Top-40 charts in order to gain fame and fortune.

1672. Stephanie Mills recreated Judy Garland's role in this Broadway musical which was a revamping of the 1939 MGM classic.

1673. They played the title roles in the 1959 film, *Porgy and Bess*.

1674. In this film, Sidney Poitier is part of a Chicago family whose poverty is disrupted by a windfall $10,000 insurance check.

1675. In this year ABC-TV aired its mini-series extravaganza, based on Alex Haley's book, *Roots*.

1676. In *Roots*, Kunta Kinte of the Mandika tribe is abducted into slavery in the 1750's from what is now this African nation.

1677. Hattie McDaniel won an Oscar for Best Supporting Actress for this 1939 film.

1678. She played Prissy in the 1939 romance, *Gone With the Wind*.

1679. Eddie Anderson appeared in this late 1946 film which was censored by a Memphis film board because star Robert Walker tipped his hat to an African-American.

1680. He was discovered at the Maple Leaf Club, had great initial success at ragtime, but died in poverty and relative obscurity.

1681. Known as one of the premier singers of romantic ballads, this vocalist originally wanted to run track in the Olympics.

1682. Turned into a vampire, William Marshall is unleashed on Los Angeles in this 1972 film.

1683. His music won an Oscar for the 1971 detective drama, *Shaft.*

1684. Gene Wilder is paired with this famous comedian in the 1976 film effort, *Silver Streak.*

1685. She plays Fidelia the maid in the 1944 film, *Since You Went Away,* about a Midwestern family whose men are off to war.

1686. This choir performed in countless films in the 1930's and 1940's, including *Slave Ship.*

1687. She performed in *Broadway Rhythm, Rhapsody in Blue,* and made her screen debut in the 1945 musical comedy, *Something to Shout About.*

1688. He portrayed Fred Sanford, a lazy junk collector on TV's "Sanford and Son."

1689. In this 1972 film, a desperate Paul Winfield is sentenced to a chain gang when he steals meat for his hungry family.

1690. He was the eligible, John Prentice, who came to dinner in 1967's *Guess Who's Coming to Dinner.*

1691. Irene Cara is well known for her portrayal of Coco, a student at Manhattan's High School of Performing Arts, in this film.

1692. Ernest Morrison played this character, the first black to appear in the "Our Gang" silent films.

1693. He played with Lena Horne in the 1943 semi-biographical film, *Stormy Weather.*

1694. These singing brothers perform in the 1934 Jimmy Durante comedy, *Strictly Dynamite.*

1695. He is familiar to television audiences as the sarcastic butler, Benson.

1696. He plays Big Daddy, with whom Shirley MacLaine falls in love in the musical film, *Sweet Charity.*

1697. She is affectionately called "Lady Day."

1698. He is famous for sporting one sequined glove and for housing a wildlife menagerie in his backyard in addition to countless hit records and videos.

1699. He wrote "Honeysuckle Rose," which Lena Horne sang in the MGM star-studded variety show, *Thousands Cheer.*

1700. Sidney Poitier teaches in a rough, London school and slowly gains his student's respect in this 1967 film.

1701. This film, starring James Earl Jones, is based on the incident of Barney Hill Postman and his white wife who claim they were taken aboard a space ship and examined medically.

1702. Said to be "the first black man to have a leading role in films," he played Tom in the 1914 silent film, *Uncle Tom's Cabin.*

1703. He played the sheriff in *Blazing Saddles.*

1704. Richard Pryor played the first black to cross the color line in auto racing, and Pam Grier played his wife, in this 1977 film.

1705. Melville Van Peebles made his directorial debut with this 1970 film about a bigot who turns black overnight.

1706. He was George Jefferson, dry cleaning store owner, and next-door neighbor to Archie Bunker, in television's "All in the Family."

1707. Film actor Clarence Muse wrote the screenplay with Langston Hughes and aided in the direction of this 1939 movie.

1708. The 1922 silent film, *Wife Hunters,* is one of the few all-black silents to be filmed on location in this Mississippi city.

1709. Shirley Jo Finney plays the title role in the NBC television movie, *Wilma,* about this young polio victim who goes on to win three gold medals as a runner in the 1960 Olympics.

1710. When James Cagney played a boxer in the 1933 film, *Winner Take All,* who played his trainer?

1711. Harry Belafonte starred in this 1959 film about life after a nuclear war in New York City, where only three people have survived: a black man, a white man, and a white woman over whom they struggle.

1712. Jannie Hoskins played this lesser-known character in numerous "Our Gang" episodes.

1713. You've seen her in *Car Wash*, and most recently as Gregory Hines' girl friend in *Runnin' Scared*.

1714. Sammy Davis, Jr., Juano Hernandez, and Louis Armstrong are jazz musicians who befriend Kirk Douglas, a struggling jazz trumpeter in this 1950 film.

1715. This Broadway star shares the screen with William Powell, Esther Williams, Judy Garland and Fred Astaire in the 1946 film, *Ziegfeld Follies*.

1716. This jazz great has performed in the films *The Glenn Miller Story*, *Hello Dolly* and *Satchmo the Great*.

1717. After many Broadway and film performances, she later went on to graduate from Georgetown University.

1718. This movie actor, director, and producer also played one of the prisoners of war in the television series, "Hogan's Heroes."

1719. Known mainly through her associations with the composing team of Burt Bacharach and Hal David, she was also in the film, *Slaves*.

1720. Before being known for authoring *Roots*, Alex Haley wrote the screenplay for this 1973 film.

1721. More known for performances in front of the camera, this man also worked behind the camera, directing *Buck and the Preacher* and *Uptown Saturday Night*.

1722. She started singing in the choir of her father's church, and went on to earn respect as the first lady of soul.

1723. She was in the film, *Cleopatra Jones* but is better known as the mother of a family living in the Chicago projects in "Good Times."

1724. He performed in *Claudine,* and *Cooley High,* and was a "sweathog" for several years on the TV series, "Welcome Back, Kotter."

1725. He plays the talented Harlem street kid, Leroy, in the TV series and the film, *Fame.*

1726. In the 1974 film, *Claudine,* she plays a welfare mother of six.

1727. The "Midnight Train to Georgia" brought this singer fame.

1728. In *For Pete's Sake,* he co-stars with the Reverend Billy Graham.

1729. This terrific tapdancer of Broadway's *Sophisticated Ladies,* also danced in the films *The Cotton Club* and *White Nights.*

1730. Featured in the films, *Car Wash, Cooley High,* and *Where's Poppa,* he was also a member of TV's "Saturday Night Live."

1731. In addition to writing the screenplay, she also wrote the songs featured in the 1972 film *Georgia, Georgia.*

1732. This 1954 movie starring Sidney Poitier and the Harlem Globetrotters centers on the basketball team's rise from obscurity to prominence as a major box office attraction.

1733. She performed in a segregated segment of the film, *Flying Down to Rio,* and sang an unforgettable rendition of the gritty song, "Remember My Forgotten Man" in *Gold Diggers of 1933.*

1734. He and his audience sing back and forth when he performs his famous scat song, "Hi-de-ho."

1735. Bill Cosby and Robert Culp play a pair of zany detectives who experience the same passions, pleasures, and vices in this 1972 film.

1736. In a cartoon, Betty Boop is captured by island cannibals and as she flees, this jazz man is seen in the background singing, "I'll be Glad When You're Dead, You Rascal You."

1737. Loretta, Niagara, Gussie, Pearl, and Willamay are just some of the countless servant's roles she played in films like 1934's *Imitation of Life.*

1738. Born in Georgia in 1932, this blind singer, composer, and pianist sang the theme song to the film, *In the Heat of the Night.*

1739. Noble Johnson appeared in minor and bit roles in over 43 Hollywood films, including the role of the monster-worshipping tribal chief of Skull Island, who kidnaps Fay Wray, in this 1933 film.

1740. Billie Holiday was one of the first blues singers to perform here in New York City.

1741. He played Piano Man, Billie Holiday's faithful but weak-willed friend in *Lady Sings the Blues.*

1742. Their characters were linked romantically in the 1972 film *Lady Sings the Blues* and the 1975 feature *Mahogany.*

1743. Billy Eckstine had a small acting role in this 1975 comedy directed by Sidney Poitier.

1744. Chuck Berry, Little Richard, Chubby Checker, Bo Diddley, The Shirelles, and Fats Domino are showcased in this 1973 documentary.

1745. In this the eighth James Bond film, the villains

include Yaphet Kotto, Julius Harris, and Geoffrey Holder as the voodoo prince.

1746. The Hall-Johnson Choir sings its spirituals in this classic film of Shangra-La.

1747. J. Rosamond Johnson, trained at the New England Conservatory of Music in Boston, and his brother James Weldon Johnson, wrote this popular song near the turn of the century.

1748. This black director also received credits for film editing in the 1969 feature, *Midnight Cowboy.*

1749. Rachel Welch plays Jugs and he plays Mother in the 1976 film, *Mother, Jugs and Speed,* about a comic private ambulance service.

1750 Marla Gibbs is well-known by TV audiences for this sassy, back-talking role on "The Jeffersons."

1751. Paul Robeson sang this popular description of the Mississippi.

1752. This limber dancer was seen in the movie and TV series *Fame,* and danced lead roles in Broadway shows like the revival of *Sweet Charity.*

1753. His awards include the ASCAP Awards' Composer of the Year for three consecutive years.

1754. She sang Martin Luther King, Jr.'s favorite gospel song, "Precious Lord, Take My Hand," after his funeral procession in 1968.

1755. What event is depicted in the Billie Holiday song, "Strange Fruit"?

1756. In what television series did Diahann Carroll play a nurse?

1757. She was the first female black to be cast in a major role on one of the network's prime time soap operas.

1758. She sang "Goldfinger," "Diamonds Are Forever," and "Moonraker" for the title tracks of those James Bond films.

1759. In the early 1960s, this ex-production line worker organized the Motown recording company.

1760. In 1963, Sidney Poitier won an Oscar for his role as a traveling vagabond who befriends a group of immigrant nuns and helps them build a missionary school.

1761. He was soulful DJ, Venus Flytrap on TV's "WKRP in Cincinnati."

1762. He made famous the phrase "Dy-no-mite!" in the 1970's sitcom "Good Times," which revealed one family's life in the Chicago projects.

1763. Once a member of the singing duo "Dawn" which backed up Tony Orlando, she can now be seen with Nell Carter on NBC's "Gim'me a Break."

1764. Among Lena Horne's Broadway appearances was a role in this musical which opened at the Imperial Theatre.

1765. Critics have noted the similarities between the rise of the fictitious musical group, Deena Jones and the Dreams, in the Broadway script *Dreamgirls*, and this real-life Motown group.

1766. Born Eleanor Gough McKay in Baltimore in 1915, this great vocalist recorded the hit "Lover Man" in 1944.

1767. At 16, she joined the Cotton Club as a dancer; in 1943, she performed what was to become her signature tune, "Stormy Weather."

1768. Geoffrey Holder directed *and* designed the fantastical costumes for this 1970's hit Broadway musical.

1769. This soul and R&B singer suffered through two tragic car crashes--one which left him crippled.

1770. He played Harlem-born-and-bred Duke Curtis in the 1964 film, *The Cool World.*

1771. She claims never to have sung a song the same way twice, playing with rhythm and phrasing like a jazz instrumentalist.

1772. Known as the "First Lady of Jazz", one of her first big breaks was singing with Chick Webb and his band at the Harlem Opera House in the mid-1930s.

1773. Marian Anderson, the first black concert artist to sing with the Metropolitan Opera in 1955, also earned this distinguished credit.

1774. Born in 1887, this concert artist broke the color bar in concert halls for black classical singers.

1775. He played Bigger Thomas in the film version of *Native Son.*

1776. This famous concert and opera singer, born in 1927, has appeared in opera houses worldwide, and received the Order of Merit of the Italian Republic.

1777. This celebrated actor on Broadway and in Hollywood was a lawyer, athlete, and leader in civil rights struggles, and a member of Phi Beta Kappa.

1778. What was the nickname of Bill Robinson, the dancer who made over 14 Hollywood movies in the 1930's?

1779. William Grant Still, accomplished composer and conductor, was the first black to lead a symphony orchestra, when he conducted this group.

1780. Known for his freestyle improvisational style, this artist was the first jazz musician to receive a Guggenheim fellowship.

1781. An early associate of Charlie Parker and Dizzy Gillespie and a pioneer in the use of modern choral backgrounds, this Brooklyn-born drummer co-wrote the "Freedom Now Suite."

1782. Lionel Hampton started as a drummer, led a big band until the 1960s, and has a special reputation as the first man to play jazz on this instrument.

1783. This blues singer who toured with Sam Cooke in his early career, also spent two years as a U.S. Army parachute jumper and was seen acting on TV shows like "Bourbon Street Beat" and "77 Sunset Strip."

1784. His most successful record was "Body and Soul," and he is the first prominent tenor saxophone soloist in jazz history.

1785. This multi-instrumentalist from Detroit was one of the first jazzmen to incorporate Middle Eastern and Asian influences into his work, using instruments like the argol and various ethnic flutes.

1786. Jazz was first recorded around this year, by musicians like Joseph "King" Oliver and Jelly Roll Morton.

1787. Affectionately called "Yardbird," this jazz great was born in Kansas City in 1920.

1788. His first professional appearance was with Dr. Frazier's Medicine Show in Pennsylvania, playing melodion and buck dancing on the back of a truck.

1789. One of the finest jazz guitarists, he became known on

52nd Street and through performances with the Washboard Rhythm Kings and the Spirits of Rhythm in the 1930s.

1790. Benny Carter, Johnny Hodges, Charlie Parker and Ornette Coleman have all contributed to the jazz world with this instrument.

1791. Singing with the Raelettes (a gospel-based back-up group) in concerts, Ray Charles released this hit in 1959.

1792. Bill Coleman and his jazz trumpet made a special appearance at this foreign dignitaries' wedding reception in 1939.

1793. His clowning and horseplay earned him his nickname and lost him his job with the Cab Calloway band.

1794. Having played in films like *The New Interns,* he is more recognized for his role on TV's "Mission Impossible" team.

1795. A statue of this jazz soprano saxophonist was erected on the French Riviera after his death.

1796. In 1946, he was cast as Daniel de Bosola in the play, *The Duchess of Malfi,* becoming the first black actor to appear in New York in a previously white role.

1797. This pianist, with a driving, rhythmic left hand and nicknamed "The Lion," helped to establish the style known as the Harlem stride.

1798. This influential jazz pianist wrote the 1920's pop hit, "Charleston."

1799. Blues singer and guitarist, he won a pardon from a Louisiana prison for murder.

1800. This New Orleans musician was the first prominent string bass soloist on jazz recordings.

1801. This bandleader/pianist, who ran a shortlived Chicago club with Louis Armstrong and Zutty Singleton, composed "Rosetta."

1802. This arranger and pianist composed the popular standard, "Take the 'A Train."

1803. He was the first black musician hired by Benny Goodman.

1804. Billie Holiday's nickname, "Lady Day," was affectionately coined by this saxophonist.

1805. It is the singing of nonsense syllables instead of words, with the syllable phrased as if it were coming from a jazz horn instead of a voice.

1806. The production in the early 1920's of Eugene O'Neill's *All God's Chillun Got Wings* was critically hailed as a landmark in the development of theatre illuminating black life, particularly because of this man's performance.

1807. *In Abraham's Bosom,* first produced at the Provincetown Theatre with Julius Bledsoe, won for playwright Paul Green this award in 1927.

1808. This playwright won the *Crisis* contest two years in a row for *The Broken Banjo* and *Boo-Black Lover* in the mid-1920's.

1809. He forgot the lyric of a song during a recording session and thereby invented "scatting."

1810. Maryland actor Ira Aldrich, unable to get serious roles in American theatre, went to England where he performed the role Othello on the London stage in this year.

1811. Produced by the NAACP in 1916, the play, *Rachel* by Angelina Grimke has this special significance.

1812. This choreographer is a pioneer in restoring the African and Caribbean heritage to American dance movement.

1813. Katherine Dunham left the professional stage after tremendous success to live in the ghetto of this Illinois city to work with disadvantaged youth.

1814. After several years off the charts, she came back in the 1980's in her 40's with "What's Love Got to Do With It?"

1815. This former model sold six million copies of her debut album by 1986, making it the best-selling LP by a black female vocalist in pop music history.

1816. This world-famous "King of the Blues" averages a hectic 300 concert dates a year.

1817. Who is the Detroit-born actress portraying high school administrator Liz MacIntyre on TV's "Room 222"?

1818. This trumpeter made history by winning Grammys in both classical *and* jazz fields.

1819. The NAACP Image Awards crowned her Entertainer of the Year for 1985.

1820. Once popular for his songs with a Carribbean beat, he won the 1985 Leonard H. Carter Humanitarian Award given by the NAACP.

1821. Billy Eckstine and Carmen McRae are both seen in this 1986 Richard Pryor film.

1822. Once married to the great Teddy Wilson, she was a fine pianist in her own right, and one of the few female artists to lead her own band.

1823. Cannonball Adderley is a star graduate from this Florida college.

1824. It was the first time in the 58-year history of the Academy Awards that three black women were nominated for Best Actress and Best Supporting Actress, and the nominees came from this 1985 film.

1825. This Chicago talk-show hostess won a Best Supporting Actress nomination for her portrayal of the strong-willed Sophia in *The Color Purple.*

1826. Veteran actress Margaret Avery played this role of the fast-living blues singer who befriends downtrodden Celie in the film, *The Color Purple.*

1827. How many black actresses have won the Academy Award's Best Supporting Actress Oscar since Hattie McDaniel in 1939?

1828. He owns two Emmies for his co-starring role on the 1960's "I Spy" series, and was a cinch to capture the award for Best Actor in a sitcom in 1985, but withdrew his name not wanting to compete with fellow actors.

1829. She was considered uncastable for five years before her Oscar-nominated role in the *The Color Purple.*

1830. This veteran rock-n-roller and evangelist discovered that his songs were often re-recorded and credited to singers like Elvis Presley or Pat Boone.

1831. Known for Broadway hits like *Ain't Supposed to Die a Natural Death,* this playwright/director/producer added options trader to his list of credits when he hit Wall Street in the 1980's.

1832. Hailing from Philadelphia, she brought the world of opera to film audiences when she starred in the successful French feature, *Diva.*

1833. Since 1975, this New York-based company provides a professional showcase for undiscovered black operatic talent.

1834. In 1939, the Daughters of the American Revolution denied this contralto permission to sing in Washington, D.C.'s Constitution Hall.

1835. In 1961, this soprano from Mississippi debuted at the Metropolitan Opera House singing Leonora in Verdi's *Il Trovatore* and received a 42-minute ovation.

1836 One of the most acclaimed artists alive today, he is often heard soloing on the harmonica.

1837. This trumpeter with the middle name of Toussaint L'Overture has a doctorate in ethnomusicology.

1838. Name the bassist who played with Horace Silver at 18 and made his reputation with Chick Corea's Return to Forever.

1839. His nickname is Jaws.

1840. Name the Mississippi Delta bluesman whose "Boogie Chillen" sold a million copies in 1948.

1841. He teamed up with another trombonist, Kai Winding, in 1954.

1842. Who is the hard-driving master drummer best known for his innovative work with John Coltrane?

1843. Blind, he would play three instruments at once.

1844. A successful crossover artist, he has won Grammy Awards as a pianist and composer, and is known for "Wade in the Water."

1845. He was pianist with the John Coltrane Quartet for five years from its inception in 1960.

1846. This superb saxophonist wrote for the Jazz Messengers and Miles Davis, then formed Weather Report.

1847. Name the big-toned sax player nicknamed "Jug."

1848. She worked with Paul Whiteman's band between 1929-1933 and became well-known for her rendition of "Rockin' Chair."

1849. In what year did Count Basie compose his band's theme song, "One O'Clock Jump"?

1850. This pianist composed the funky "Moanin" and "Dat Dere" for the Jazz Messengers.

1851. *Night in Tunisia* is considered one of the finest albums produced by this veteran drummer and combo leader.

1852. Known for thumping, hypnotic chord changes, this pianist is known for the albums, *Sahara, Expansions,* and *Enlightenment.*

1853. He was a jazz trumpeter who played for Art Blakey from 1958 to 1961 and composed the "Sidewinder."

1854. His culturally relevant album, *We Insist! Freedom Now Suite* is believed to have contributed to this drummer's five-year blacklist from the recording studios in the 1960's.

1855. Name the masterly tenor saxophonist who produced the classic album, *Way Out West.*

1856. A superb composer, he co-founded the Jazz Messengers with Art Blakey.

1857. Many term him the greatest jazz vocalist; his first

name is Hezekiah.

1858. Born Sonny Blount, he explored exotic compositions with his Solar Arkestra.

1859. Name the blind harmonica player and blues singer who teamed up with Blind Boy Fuller while in his teens.

1860. Lead singer Randy Lewis died on the morning that the Drifters recorded this 1964 song.

1861. Name the group that recorded "My True Story" on the Beltone label.

1862. Berry Gordy formed Tammie Records in 1960 and renamed the company what?

1863. Sam Cooke and his manager, J.W. Alexander, formed this recording company in Hollywood.

1864. Name the original lead singer for the Four Tops.

1865. How many top ten records did the Supremes produce from 1964 to 1969?

1866. Who recorded the 1960 hit, "Ooh Poo Pah Doo"?

1867. One of the pioneers of bebop, he wore outlandish hats and composed "Mysterioso."

1868. The team of Holland-Dozier-Holland produced records by what Motown group?

1869. In 1963, at age 12, he recorded "Fingertips."

1870. Who recorded "Can I Change My Mind?" the 1969 hit?

1871. "I Found A Love" was recorded by the Falcons in 1962 with this singer as lead.

1872. This jazz trumpeter was born in Philadelphia and shot dead outside a New York City club, Slugs.

1873. This blues-based percussive pianist has contributed classics like "Doodlin'," "The Preacher," "Señor Blues" and "Song for My Father."

1874. A New Thing tenor and soprano saxophonist, he is fiercely political, producing "Things Have Got to Change" and "Attica Blues."

1875. Jazz's best-known organist, he recorded "A Walk on the Wild Side" for Verve.

1876. Born in Dallas, this fierce trumpet player and hoarse singer began his career with Ma Rainey's band.

1877. Considered a virtuoso pianist, this jazz great made a sensational debut in 1949 at a Carnegie Hall Jazz at the Philharmonic concert.

1878. Acknowledged by many as bebop's greatest pianist, he settled in Paris in 1959 and produced *Our Man in Paris* with Dexter Gordon.

1879. This master of the polyrhythmic and cymbal beat, he was Charlie Parker's drummer from 1946-48.

1880. In 1958, this saxophonist's composition, "The Freedom Suite" was reissued as "The Shadow Waltz" because of its reference to African-American equality.

1881. Grouped with the New Thing tenor players, this jazz artist is known for screaming clusters of notes and Om-type mantras in the background.

1882. Name the percusssion player who composed the frequently recorded "Afro-Blue."

1883. This pianist-composer died in a mental institution in 1917.

1884. He is one of the first jazz saxophonists to incorporate Middle Eastern and Asian influnces in his work.

1885. This bluesman's real name is Peter Chatman.

1886. What pianist-composer fronted the Red Hot Peppers in 1926?

1887. This bebop trumpeter died of TB and addiction at age 26.

1888. Touted as the *"Mother of the Blues,"* this vocalist made her first public appearance at age 12 in the vaudeville show, *Bunch of Blackberries.*

1889. What jazz saxophonist recorded the soundtrack for the movie, *Alfie?*

1890. What famous jazz saxophonist had his greatest success with his first album, *Them Dirty Blues?*

1891. This instrumentalist and vocalist was born in 1900 and was an orphan raised at the Cresent City's Coloured Waifs Home.

1892. Who composed "I'm Just Wild About Harry," Harry Truman's 1948 presidential campaign song?

1893. What jazz trumpet soloist is known as "Little Jazz"?

1894. This jazz singer conducted Chick Webb's orchestra after his death.

1895. What jazz pianist wrote the standard, "Misty"?

1896. What jazz trumpeter made the beret, horn-rim glasses and goatee the bebop uniform?

1897. This child prodigy performed Mozart Piano Concertos with the Chicago Symphony Orchestra at age 11.

1898. What urban blues "shouter" was known as "Mr. Five By Five"?

1899. This musician was the first jazz banjoist to attain a reputation.

1900. In 1942, this group had one of the first big hits by a black band with "Choo Choo Ch'Boogie."

1901. At age 14, she toured with Ma Rainey's Rabbit Foot Minstrels.

1902. This pianist established the style known as Harlem stride.

1903. What composer of "Lush Life" was the closest collaborator of Duke Ellington?

1904. What big bluesman popularized "Shake Rattle & Roll" long before Bill Haley and the Comets?

1905. She is the "Divine One."

1906. What pianist-composer-vocalist appeared in the movie, *Stormy Weather?*

1907. Because of her height and thinness, this jazz songstress was known as "Sweet Mama Stringbean."

1908. This blues guitarist-harmonica player and vocalist's real name is McKinley Morganfield.

1909. This jazz pianist was influenced by beboppers who frequented his Brooklyn restaurant.

1910. Because of her composing, arranging and piano

playing, she is called the First Lady of Jazz.

1911. In the late 1930's, Billie Holiday forged a partnership with what famous sax-man?

1912. This ballad-singing group was described by Decca Records as "five boys and a guitar."

1913. What is the title of the Orioles' first rhythm and blues hit?

1914. The Spaniels, on the Vee Jay label, had a success with this tune in 1954.

1915. Bobby Lester sang lead for this Moonglows hit on the Chess label.

1916. For what group did Nate Wilson sing "I'll Be Home" in 1954?

1917. Name the lead singer for most of the recordings by the Platters.

1918. Name the lead singer with the 'fifties rhythm and blues group, the Orioles.

1919. This singer's biggest success was "Jim Dandy."

1920. This rhythm and blues group hit it big in 1953 with their tune, "Crying in the Chapel."

1921. Eugene Mumford was the lead singer for this group which recorded "My Reverie" in 1951.

1922. Who sang lead for the Five Kings on their 1951 success, "Glory of Love"?

1923. Who wrote the Spaniels' 1954 hit and was their lead singer also?

1924. The Moonglows used this name when recording on the Chess Label.

1925. The Platters recorded this tune in 1953 for Federal Records.

1926. LaVern Baker's hit "Tweedle Dee" was recorded in what year?

1927. This singer was the third lead for the Chicago group, the Flamingos, in the late 'fifties.

1928. Who sang "Life is But a Dream" and "A Sunday Kind of Love"?

1929. The first hit on Atlantic for this group from Washington, D.C. was "Don't You Know I Love You."

1930. Who sang lead for the Five Satins 1956 recording, "(I'll Remember) In the Still of the Night"?

1931. This 'fifties hit was sung by the Chants.

1932. Name the big touring band which was called a "Rhythm and Blues Caravan."

1933. Who recorded "No Rollin' Blues" in 1949?

1934. Her recording of "5-10-15 Hours" in 1952 featured a tenor solo by Willis Jackson.

1935. He was a pioneer in the use of the electric guitar as a stage prop.

1936. Roy Milton's recording of this tune in 1945 was the first to reach sales of more than a million copies in the African-American market.

1937. What was Ike Turner's jump band called?

1938. Name the singer in the B.B. King-led band, the Beale Streeters.

1939. His first record at age 17, "The Fat Man," was one of the biggest rhythm and blues hits of 1949.

1940. His biggest hit was his first record in 1952, "Lawdy, Miss Clawdy."

1941. A New Orleans singer with a gospel style, he recorded "The Things That I Used to Do" in 1954.

1942. Name the tune by Ivory Joe Hunter which sold over a million copies in 1950.

1943. The influential "Please Send Me Someone to Love" was recorded in 1950 by whom?

1944. He was one of Aristocrat/Chess Records best-selling recording artists, releasing "Hoochie Coochie" in 1950.

1945. One of the few guitar-playing woman blues singers, she recorded the 1962 success, "You'll Lose A Good Thing."

1946. Minit Records was founded by this producer in New Orleans in 1960.

1947. Bobby Marchan's 1960 hit, "There is Something On Your Mind" was adapted from a hit the previous year by whom?

1948. Who was the lead singer for the Drifters on "Dance With Me"?

1949. A native of Laurel, Mississippi, she began piano lessons at age four and was called the "voice of the century."

1950. This graduate of Wayne State University became the leading male singer among black operatic stars in the

1960's.

1951. He was the first black man to be appointed to a permanent position as a symphony orchestra conductor in the United States in 1968.

1952. When the Rochester Philharmonic Symphony performed his *Afro-American Symphony* in 1931, this gentleman began to be recognized as one of our greatest American composers.

1953. The Dominoes' first recording hit, this tune featured the bass, Bill Brown.

1954. He was the first black American to conduct a white radio orchestra in the nation when he conducted WNBC's Deep River orchestra in 1930.

1955. In 1955, she became the first African-American to star in an opera on television when she appeared in Puccini's *Tosca*.

1956. He became the first African-American male to obtain a permanent association with the Metropolitan Opera.

1957. One of the first blacks to prepare for a career conducting symphony orchestras, he took a permanent position with the Goteborg Symphony in Sweden.

1958. In 1961, she received a 42-minute standing ovation at the Metropolitan Opera House after singing Leonora in Verdi's *Ll Trovatore*.

1959. This 50-voice all-black music group won fame during the Second World War and was conducted by Leonard De Paur.

1960. Name the famous Harlem nightclub on West 118th Street which nurtured the birth of bebop.

1961. His album, *The Birth of the Cool,* was this trumpeter's important contribution to the cool jazz movement after bebop.

1962. The leading figure of the avant garde jazz movement of the 1950's, this alto saxophonist was the first jazz musician to receive a Guggenheim Fellowship.

1963. Bandleader, arranger, composer, he wrote the score for the film, *The Pawnbroker* and for the television series, *Ironside.*

1964. In 1954, the first jazz festival in the United States was held in this town.

1965. A National Negro Opera Company which presented Verdi's *Aida* at the Chicago Opera House in 1942 was organized by this woman.

1966. A pioneer principal black singer for the New York City Opera Company in 1946, he sang in Leoncavallo's *Pagliacci.*

1967. Who recorded the top ten hits, "This Magic Moment" and "Save the Last Dance For Me" in 1960?

1968. This top ten hit in 1963 was recorded by the Chiffons before "One Fine Day" of the same year.

1969. This country and western song was a success for Ray Charles in 1962.

1970. Three top black ballad singers died violently in the 1960's -- Johnny Ace, Sam Cooke and this man.

1971. Formerly with the Pilgrim Travellers, he sang a duet with Sam Cooke on "Bring it on Home to Me."

1972. Name the gospel-influenced ballad singer of the 'fifties who would tear off his clothes for his audience.

1973. He recorded the first rhythm and blues rendition of "Unchained Melody" in 1955.

1974. Name the Drifters' first recorded song.

1975. He was the lead singer for the Five Royales.

1976. "Work With Me, Annie" was recorded by what group?

1977. "Please, Please, Please" was the big hit by James Brown and the Famous Flames in what year?

1978. The twist dance style was conceived by this singer whose recordings of the same name sold more than a million copies in the black community.

1979. Name the vocal group of which Gary "U.S. Bonds" was a member before recording "School is Out."

1980. Name the lead singer for the Midnighters.

1981. Huey Smith and the Clowns first recorded this song describing a popular 1960's dance.

1982. Who recorded "A Million to One" in 1961?

1983. He served as the composer-in-residence for the Negro Ensemble Company.

1984. The Five Blind Boys of Mississippi recorded for what Houston-based record label?

1985. A New York gospel singing instructor, Billy Ward, formed this rhythm and blues group in 1950.

1986. Who was the lead singer for the Dominoes for their hit, "The Bells"?

1987. Who replaced singer Clyde McPhatter when he left the Dominoes for another group?

1988. Who wrote "Got a Job" and "Bad Girls" for the Miracles?

1989. Clyde McPhatter left the Dominoes to form this group.

1990. After leaving the Drifters, Ben E. King first recorded this song.

1991. She was lead singer in the all-woman vocal group, the Shirelles.

1992. On what label did the Miracles record "Shop Around" in 1961?

1993. Who recorded "Daddy's Home" in 1961?

1994. In 1957, Juggy Murray formed this record company which released songs by Ike and Tina Turner.

1995. Hank Ballard, Little Willie John and Jackie Wilson were discovered at a 1951 talent show by whom?

1996. This group was the most commercially successful of all Motown entertainers.

1997. What is Sly Stone's real name?

1998. How many songs did Fats Domino have on the rhythm and blues top ten lists during the 1955-60 period?

1999. Name the firm established to publish the materials written by Berry Gordy and Smokey Robinson.

ANSWERS

ANSWERS

1. Jamestown, VA ⌐

2. David Bunt

3. Thomas Cox Allen ✓

4. David Ruggles

5. James Russell Dumpson

6. W.E.B. DuBois

7. 1916

8. Alain L. Locke ✓

9. 1619 ✓

10. 1638

11. *Desire*

12. Massachusetts

13. Corn planter

14. Maryland ⌐

15. The Society of Friends

16. Elias Neau

17. Crispus Attucks ⌐

18. Lunsford Land

19. Jean Baptiste Point ⌐ DuSable

20. Henry Blair ⌐

21. Vermont ✓

22. George Washington

23. Freedom

24. *The Declaration of Independence*

25. Silver Bluff, S. C.

26. Andrew J. Beard

27. The National Negro Business League

28. John Merrick

29. Philadelphia

30. The Northwest Territory

31. Benjamin Banneker

32. January 1, 1808

33. The Freedmen's Savings Bank

34. 1810

35. Denmark Vesey

36. Alexander Lucius Twilight

37. *Freedom's Journal*

38. James Augustine Healy

39. Louis Howard Latimer

40. Isaiah T. Montgomery

41. 1830

42. Benjamin Banneker

43. "Jenny Coupler"

44. Richard Allen

45. Nat Turner

46. 40

47. The Liberty Party

48. Elijah McCoy

49. The Haynes Razor Strop

50. Blanche Kelso Bruce

51. Macon B. Allen

52. Three

53. Harriet Tubman

54. "The Real McCoy"

55. *Black Enterprise*

56. Herman Perry

57.	William C. Nell	73.	Patrick Francis ∨ Healy
58.	Martin R. Delany	74.	The Black Codes
59.	The Kansas-Nebraska Act	75.	1866 ·
60.	The Dred Scott ∨ decision	76.	Alexandria, VA ·
61.	An Adding Machine	77.	The Ku Klux Klan ✓
62.	Jan E. Matzelinger ✓	78.	Garrett A. Morgan ∨
63.	EDP Audit Controls Inc.	79.	1964
64.	Oscar James Dunn	80.	William Alexander Leidesdorff
65.	The Second Confiscation Act	81.	Francis L. Cardozo
66.	The Emancipation ∨ Proclamation	82.	Oscar J. Dunn
67.	*The North Star* ✓	83.	Jonathan Jasper Wright
68.	Sgt. William H. ✓ Carney	84.	Hiram R. Revels ✓
69.	The *New Orleans Tribune*	85.	Norbert Rillieux
70.	January 31, 1865 ✓	86.	Charlotte E. Ray ✓
71.	Independence Bank of Chicago	87.	John Henry Conyers ✓
72.	Oscar James Dunn	88.	Patrick Francis ✓ Healy
		89.	Yale
		90.	Henry O. Flipper ✓

91.	1898	110.	*Baltimore Afro-American*
92.	Tuskegee Institute		
		111.	Charles V. Richley
93.	Tennessee		
		112.	1915
94.	John R. Lynch		
		113.	Cosmetics
95.	Washington, D.C.		
		114.	26
96.	Provident Hospital		
		115.	*The Mirror of Liberty*
97.	Joseph Blair		
98.	Emmet J. Rice	116.	1914
99.	Dr. Daniel Hale Williams	117.	1921
		118.	1923
100.	The National Medical Association	119.	Carter G. Woodson
101.	*Plessy vs. Ferguson*	120.	National Bar Association
102.	Maggie L. Walker		
		121.	26%
103.	Scovel Richardson		
		122.	Arthur L. Mitchell
104.	Thomy Lafon		
		123.	1938
105.	The NAACP		
		124.	Jane Matilda Bolin
106.	W.E.B. DuBois		
		125.	Percy L. Julian
107.	Baltimore, MD		
		126.	Asa T. Spaulding
108.	Woodrow Wilson		
		127.	Wholesale food supplies
109.	William A. Hinton		

128. North Carolina Mutual Life of Durham

129. William A. Leidesdorff

130. Benjamin Oliver Davis, Sr.

131. Crystal Bird Fauset

132. The Congress of Racial Equality

133. Louis Howard Latimer

134. Charles Clinton Spaulding

135. 1945

136. Wesley A. Brown

137. Harry Truman

138. Atlanta, GA

139. Edith Sampson

140. Granville T. Woods

141. William Monroe Trotter

142. Ralph J. Bunche

143. Cicero

144. 1952

145. Three years

146. Lloyd A. Hall

147. *Pittsburgh Courier*

148. *Brown vs. Board of Education*

149. Benjamin O. Davis, Jr.

150. Rosa Parks

151. Martin Luther King, Jr.

152. W. Robert Ming

153. Granville T. Woods

154. Dr. Joseph Edison Walker

155. John W. Barfield, Sr.

156. New York City

157. Student Non-Violent Coordinating Committee

158. Elijah Muhammed

159. Granville T. Woods

160. James H. Meredith

161. Sixteenth Street Baptist Church

162. Medgar W. Evers

163. Malcolm X

164. Martin Luther King, Jr.

165. Henry E. Baker

166. Carter Walker Wesley

167. Jan Matzelinger

168. William Alexander Leidesdorff

169. Syphilis

170. *The Mirror of Liberty*

171. Malcolm X

172. Patricia R. Harris

173. A derrick

174. Stokely Carmichael

175. Constance Baker Motley

176. James Forten

177. National Negro Business League

178. Bobby Seale

179. 43

180. Lucius D. Amerson

181. Virginia

182. Thurgood Marshall

183. James Forten

184. Catering

185. 1975

186. Major Robert H. Lawrence, Jr.

187. Carl B. Stokes

188. Yvonne Clark

189. Dorothy Bolden

190. Mary Mattie Smith

191. Joseph Searles III

192. Thelma Dailey

193. Margaret Bush Wilson

194. Howard University

195.	Rev. Channing E. Phillips	**211.**	Thomas B. Dalton
196.	Rep. Shirley Chisholm	**212.**	Andrew F. Brimmer
197.	Norbert Rillieux	**213.**	1960
198.	Anthony Johnson	**214.**	Yvonne Braithwaite Burke
199.	Rep. Parren Mitchell	**215.**	Barbara Jordan
200.	Mark Clark	**216.**	P.B.S. Pinchback
201.	People United to Save Humanity	**217.**	Airships
		218.	Tailor
202.	Clifford Alexander, Jr.	**219.**	Kenneth C. Younger
203.	Norbert Rillieux		
		220.	James Derham
204.	Andrew Young		
		221.	James Hall
205.	Clifton R. Wharton, Sr.		
		222.	John V. DeGrasse
206.	James Weldon Johnson	**223.**	Edward A. Bouchet
		224.	Lewis Adams
207.	Robert C. Weaver		
		225.	Thomas J. Carter
208.	Ebenezer Don Carlos Bassett	**226.**	W.E.B. DuBois
209.	Coca-Cola Bottling Company	**227.**	1944
		228.	Benjamin Banneker
210.	Louis H. Latimer		

229.	W.E.B. DuBois	248.	Arthur Teele
230.	The Bible	249.	William C. Prior
231.	World War I	250.	Mayor
232.	Claude McKay	251.	D. Michael Cheers
233.	Harry S. Truman	252.	Dr. A.H. McCoy
234.	100%	253.	1984
235.	Frederick Douglass	254.	HUD secretary
236.	Louisiana	255.	Patricia R. Harris
237.	Dorothy Tillman	256.	Katie Hall
238.	Lionel J. Wilson	257.	The Lutheran Church
239.	20	258.	Jimmy Carter
240.	Seven	259.	Mwlina Imiri Abubadika
241.	Booker T. Washington	260.	FBI
242.	Elizabeth Keckley	261.	17
243.	Six	262.	Detroit Urban League
244.	Lemuel B. Haynes	263.	John H. Burton
245.	Atlanta University	264.	Richmond, CA
246.	*The Philadelphia Tribune*	265.	Seven
247.	Robert Clark	266.	Hugh N. Mulzac

267. Adam Clayton Powell, Jr.

268. Donald Reeves

269. Homer Smith

270. Dr. Samuel Nabrit

271. Carlotta A. Bass

272. Shirley Chisholm

273. Black Panther Party

274. Malcolm Little

275. Howard N. Lee

276. Dayton, Ohio

277. E. Frederick Morrow

278. Philippa Schuyler

279. 214

280. Lyndon Johnson

281. Kenneth B. Clark

282. 18.9%

283. Gary, Indiana

284. Daniel P. Moynihan

285. Nathaniel Bates

286. Cincinnati, Ohio

287. 6%

288. Richard Nixon

289. Massachusetts

290. Boston

291. Harlem Prep

292. Wilberforce University

293. University of Missouri Law School

294. 1%

295. President Kennedy

296. The Black Muslims

297. James L. Usry

298. Joseph Addabbo

299. A Better Chance (ABC)

300. *Christian Recorder*

301. Alpha Kappa Alpha Sorority

302. Alpha Phi Alpha Fraternity, Inc.

303. 1933

304. Ancient Egyptian Arabic Order Nobles Mystic Shrine, Inc. (AEAONMS)

305. Nursing

306. Prince Hall

307. Congressional Black Caucus

308. Howard University

309. *Improved Benevolent Protective Order of Elks of the World*

310. Kappa Alpha Psi Fraternity, Inc.

311. A supreme being

312. The NAACP

313. 27

314. Metropolitan Museum of Art

315. National Urban League

316. Omega Psi Phi Fraternity

317. The Black Muslims

318. University of Alabama

319. Very Rev. Harold R. Perry

320. France

321. 1915

322. Wyatt Tee Walker

323. Watts

324. Louis Lomax

325. Pettis Perry

326. William J. Allen

327. Joel A. Rogers

328. John Russwurm

329. Nicolas Biddle

330. Lloyd Sealy

331. Mrs. Ruth Hall Thomas

332. Mrs. Gertrude Elise Ayer

333. *New York Freeman*

334. John H. Johnson

335. Sadie T.M. Alexander

336. Ida B. Wells Barnett

337. Kenneth Allen Gibson

338. Daisy Bates

339. Benjamin Jefferson Davis

340. Hallie Q. Brown

341. Nannie Helen Burroughs

342. Dr. Anna Julia Cooper

343. The National Council of Negro Women

344. Marjorie Lawson

345. Bob Harrison

346. Dr. Jeanne Noble

347. Benetta B. Washington

348. Alabama's

349. 1968

350. Southern Christian Leadership Conference

351. Louis H. Patterson, Jr.

352. 46

353. Cornell University

354. Rev. Ralph D. Abernathy

355. Antioch College

356. James M. Nabrit, Jr.

357. Benjamin F. Chavers, Jr.

358. William A. Hinton

359. A. Leon Higginbotham, Jr.

360. Rev. Henry Jogner, Jr.

361. Dr. Hugh H. Scott

362. Ford Motor Company

363. Judge Garrity

364. The Lost-Found

Nation of Islam in
the Wilderness of
North America

365.   Ensign Jesse Leroy
        Brown

366.   Baltimore

367.   Ford Foundation

368.   Louisiana State
        University

369.   Benjamin L. Hooks

370.   Dick Gregory

371.   Robert Wedgeworth

372.   Frederick E.
        Davidson

373.   Angela Davis

374.   Frank Willis   ↻

375.   Daniel "Chappie" ✓
        James'

376.   Soul City

377.   70%

378.   Brigadier General

379.   1973

380.   National Black
        Network

381.   Rev. Dr. Lawrence
        W. Bottoms

382.   IQ tests

383.   Dr. Percy L. Julian

384.   Chicago, Illinois

385.   John Hope
        Franklin

386.   Meharry Medical
        College

387.   Rev. Dr. Joseph H.
        Evans

388.   1976

389.   American Chemical
        Society

390.   Chicago

391.   Joanne Little

382.   Five

393.   38

394.   Interracial couples

395.   Booker T.
        Washington

396.   Estevan(ico)

397.   James P.

Beckwourth

398. Matthew Henson ✓

399. Free African Society

400. The Milton House Museum

401. Isaiah Dorman

402. Cornelius A. Scott

403. John Herman Henry Sengstacke

404. 1969

405. Richard G. Hatcher ✓

406. Maynard Jackson

407. Fannie Lou Hamer

408. Los Angeles, California ✓

409. Adam Clayton Powell, Jr. ✓

410. Charles W. Anderson

411. Abyssinian Baptist Church

412. Arthur A. Schomburg

413. San Francisco Metro Group

414. *The Crisis*

415. *The North Star*

416. Adam Clayton Powell, Jr.

417. Alain Locke ✓

418. Claude McKay

419. Julian Mayfield

420. Hoyt W. Fuller

421. *Black World*

422. George Moses Horton

423. 1944

424. Eight

425. Henry M. Collins

426. Cheney State ✓ Training School

427. Samuel Lee Gravely, Jr. ✓

428. Mary Jane Patterson

429. Arthur Herndon

430. Ida Gray Nelson
Rollins

431. Nimrod B. Allen

432. Pittsburgh, PA

433. 1940

434. Floyd B. McKissick

435. Hazel Johnson

436. *Atlanta World*

437. Jerome H. Holland

438. Marian Wright
Edelman

439. Sgt. Adolphus
Samms

440. Otis Boykin

441. Gloria Dean Scott

442. Anthony Overton

443. William A. Booth

444. B. L. Jordan

445. Ida B. Wells-
Barnett

446. Sgt. Adolphus
Samms

447. Autherine Lucy

448. Pennsylvania

449. 1967

450. Aileen Hernandez

451. David N. Croswait,
Jr.

452. Ella Mae Collins

453. Kathleen Cleaver

454. Elaine Brown

455. Robert Cheesboro

456. Florence M. Rice

457. Douglass College

458. W. W. Browne

459. North Carolina
Mutual and
Provident
Association

460. Free African
Society

461. Thomas Forten

462. Joesph Cassey

463. Gabriel Prosser

464. *Liberator*

465. Nivelle Beaubien

466. Dr. George F. Grant

467. Marcus Garvey

468. George Baker

469. Newport Gardner

470. The African Methodist Episcopal Church (AME)

471. Liberia

472. *Ebony*

473. Benjamin Banneker

474. Glaucoma

475. David Walker

476. 1849

477. Ashmam Institute

478. Martin R. Delaney

479. 1865

480. Rev. W. R. Pettiford

481. Chesapeake Marine Railroad and Dry Dock Co.

482. William Still

483. James Tate

484. Greenfield Bus Body Company

485. Oxford, PA

486. John Brown

487. Mildred Blount

488. James Stone

489. John S. Rock

490. 1866

491. Greenfield Bus Body Company

492. William Wormley

493. Wiley Jones

494. 1868

495. Paul Gaines

496. Maurice W. Lee, Sr.

497. Mary Church Terrell

498. 1918

499. Barber shop

500.	Hotel Berry	**517.**	Jo Anderson
501.	Sam Charles	**518.**	Clarence Reed White
502.	Southern Aid Society	**519.**	Lyndon Johnson
503.	Frederick Douglass	**520.**	The Economic Opportunity Act
504.	The Trade Union Corp.	**521.**	John Mitchell
505.	*Gibbs vs Board of Education*	**522.**	R. B. Fitzgerald
		523.	John B. Nail
506.	1951	**524.**	Jesse B. Blayton
507.	Mary E. Burwell	**525.**	Louis Howard Latimer
508.	John Mullen		
509.	Fisk University	**526.**	Los Angeles, CA
510.	1953	**527.**	James Derham
511.	E. Franklin Frazier	**528.**	Cotton
512.	Aero foam	**529.**	Oakland, CA ✓
513.	Emmett Till ✓	**530.**	Charles R. Drew ✓
514.	The Southern ✓ Christian Leadership Conference	**531.**	Edward W. Brooke ✓
		532.	1968
		533.	Samuel B. Fuller
515.	1957	**534.**	Elijah McCoy ✓
516.	Percy Julian		

535. Hyram S. Thomas

536. Lyndon Johnson

537. Three

538. Five

539. 1928

540. 1970

541. 1971

542. Edward Davis

543. Arkansas

544. 1971

545. Saratoga chip

546. 1924

547. 43

548. Ena Hartman

549. Augustus Jackson

550. 1971

551. The Ford Foundation

552. Carl T. Rowan

553. 1971

554. Cephus Hauser

555. Player piano

556. William H. Hastie ✓

557. James A. Bland

558. 1965

559. William B. Purvis

560. Eleanor Holmes Norton

561. 1924

562. The United Negro College Fund

563. Solomon Harper

564. Two

565. Otis Boykin

566. Louis Franklin

567. 57

568. Grambling, Louisiana

569. 1928

570. W.E.B. DuBois

571. Donald Lopes

572. An Ultraviolet Camera/Spectograph

573. Nashville, Tennesse ✓

574. Philadelphia

575. Samuel Fraunces

576. Atlanta, Georgia ✓

577. Barney Ford

578. Junius Graves

579. James Brown

580. Atlanta, Georgia

581. Richmond, Virginia

582. A.G. Gaston

583. Seaway National Bank of Chicago

584. Tougaloo, Mississppi

585. Abram Harris

586. New Orleans, Louisiana

587. George Washington Carver

588. The National Association of Colored Women

589. Rape

590. *The Negro As Capitalist*

591. Thomy Lafon

592. Radio City Music Hall ✓

593. The National Council of Negro Women

594. Social Security

595. Dorie Miller ✓

596. The American Red Cross

597. The True Reformers Bank

598. Mrs. St. Charles Lockett

599. Frederick McKinley Jones ✓

600. Detroit

601. Chicago

602. W.D. Fard ✓

603. Philadelphia, Mississippi

604. March 17, 1965

605.	Mary Eliza Mahoney	**621.**	Thomas Downing
606.	Sidney L. Kauntz	**622.**	Philadelphia
607.	July 2, 1964	**623.**	Capital Savings Bank
608.	1888	**624.**	*The Crisis of the Negro Intellectual*
609.	Algiers		
610.	Angela Davis	**625.**	Grumman International
611.	Mississippi	**626.**	Harold Washington
612.	Lewis Temple's	**627.**	28
613.	Anatomy and Physical Anthropology	**628.**	Church and fraternal groups
614.	Assistant Secretary of Labor	**629.**	Solomon Humphries
		630.	New York
615.	George Edwin	**631.**	Henry Topp
616.	Broadside Press	**632.**	M.R. DeMortie
617.	O.S. "Ozzie" Williams	**633.**	Wilson Goode
618.	Ernest Morial	**634.**	John M. Langston
619.	Founders Savings and Loan Association	**635.**	J.H. Lewis
		636.	Coleman Young
620.	Providence, Rhode Island	**637.**	Frederick M. Jones

638. Mary Berry

639. Granville T. Woods

640. Anne Lowe

641. Anne Thompson

642. Constance Iona Slaughter

643. Newburger, Loeb and Co.

644. Joan S. Wallace

645. Unita Blackwell

646. Barbara Watson

647. Susan Smith McKinney Steward

648. 65

649. 1970

650. 1,051

651. Martha Franklin

652. General Electric ✓

653. Barry Beckham

654. Carl B. Stokes

655. Marcus Garvey ✓

656. 29

657. Springfield, Illinois

658. 369th Colored Infantry

659. Nat Love ✓

660. Oscar De Priest ✓

661. The National Black United Front

662. Loretta Thompson Glickman

663. Amalya Lyle Kearse

664. William Still

665. 311

666. Donald C. Walker

667. *Black Manhattan*

668. George W. Williams

669. *Men of Mark*

670. Eleanor Holmes Norton

671. William H. Gray, III

672. Julius W. Hobson

673.	Charles C. Diggs, Jr.	*689.*	George Henry White
674.	U.W. Clemon	*690.*	Mary Church Terrell
675.	Donald F. McHenry	*691.*	Gus Savage
676.	Martin R. Delaney	*692.*	Mary McLeod Bethune
677.	Bernard Harleston	*693.*	Dr. Frederick Patterson
678.	Charlotte Scott		
679.	Henry McNeal Turner	*694.*	Walter White
680.	Peter H. Clark	*695.*	A. Philip Randolph
681.	Richard T. Greener	*696.*	James B. Parsons
682.	John P. Green	*697.*	Henry McNeal Turner
683.	George Edwin Taylor	*698.*	Augustus F. Hawkins
684.	Rev. Fred Shuttlesworth	*699.*	Alabama
685.	E. Frederic Morrow	*700.*	Barbara Jordan
686.	Brig. Gen. Sherian G. Cadoria	*701.*	George L. Brown
687.	Dr. Charles S. Johnson	*702.*	Gen. Daniel "Chappie" James
688.	Charles H. Mahoney	*703.*	Franklin A Thomas
		704.	Constance Baker Motley

705. Walter E. Washington

706. Rev. Walter Fauntroy

707. Vernon E. Jordan

708. Joseph W. Hatchett

709. John T. Walker

710. Mabel Murphy Smythe

711. J. Raymond Jones

712. Five

713. Patricia Roberts Harris

714. Milton Olive, Jr.

715. Mrs. Robert W. Claytor

716. U.S. Solicitor General

717. Jewel Lafontant

718. W. Sterling Cary

719. North Carolina A&T

720. Daisy Bates

721. Earl B. Dickerson

722. Dr. Benjamin Mays

723. William L. Dawson

724. Andrew Hatcher

725. Dr. Walter Massey

726. A. J. Cooper

727. Samuel Lee Gravely, Jr.

728. Charles Rangel

729. Parren J. Mitchell

730. George Davis

731. Richard C. Erwin

732. Theodore R. Newman, Jr.

733. Clarence Thomas

734. Mervyn M. Dymally

735. Major R. Owens

736. Louis Stokes

737. Christopher F. Edley

738. Rev. Joseph E. Lowery

739. A. Leon Higginbotham

740. Wilson Riles

741. Johnny L. Ford

742. Marion S. Barry, Jr.

743. Floyd B. McKissick

744. Gayraud S. Wilmore

745. Rhode Island

746. Frank Snowden

747. Julius LeVonne Chambers

748. Louis Stokes

749. Frank E. Peterson, Jr.

750. James Frank

751. Arnette R. Hubbard

752. Robert C. Maynard

753. Robert O. Goodman, Jr.

754. John Mercer Langston

755. National Association for the Advancement of Colored People

756. W.E.B. DuBois

757. Claude Brown

758. Edward Bannister

759. *Under the Oaks*

760. Edmonia Lewis

761. *The Flagellants*

762. Henry Ossawa Tanner

763. Henry Ossawa Tanner

764. *Black Macho & the Myth of the Superwoman*

765. *African Dancer*

766. Gayl Jones

767. Jupiter Hammon

768. Four

769. Frederick Douglass

770. *The Interesting Narrative of the Life*

of Olaudah Equiano, or Gustavus Vassa

771. David Walker

772. Eugene Warbourg

773. *The Big Sea*

774. *God's Trombones: Seven Negro Sermons in Verse*

775. *Cane*

776. Albery A. Whitman

777. *Native Son*

778. James Baldwin

779. *Invisible Man*

780. Max Reddick

781. Imamu Amiri Baraka

782. Scipio Moorehead

783. Blacksmithing

784. Nova Scotia

785. Robert S. Duncanson

786. Works Progress Administration

787. Edmonia Lewis

788. Richard Wright

789. The Harmon Foundation

790. Hale Woodruff

791. Howard University

792. Jacob Lawrence

793. Horace Pippin

794. "Outhouse" school

795. Bob Thompson

796. Abstract Expressionists

797. Senegal

798. Aaron Miller

799. Phillis Wheately

800. London

801. James A. Porter

802. Louisiana

803. Paul Lawrence Dunbar

804. Edmonia Lewis

805. Claude McKay

806. Mary Todd Lincoln

807. *The Conjure Woman*

808. Jupiter Hammon

809. *Narrative of Frederick Douglass, an American Slave, Written by Himself*

810. William Wells Brown

811. Booker T. Washington

812. *The Sport of the Gods*

813. William Edouard Scott

814. Zora Neale Hurston

815. Works Progress Administration

816. *James Baldwin*

817. *For Colored Girls Who Have Considered the Rainbow When Suicide Wasn't Enuf*

818. Milkman

819. William Stanley Braithwaite

820. James Weldon Johnson

821. *Uncle Remus: His Songs and Sayings*

822. Jesse B. Simple

823. Lucy Terry

824. Alice Dunbar Nelson's

825. *The Fledgling Bard and the Poetry Society*

826. George Moses Horton

827. James M. Whitfield

828. *Poems on Miscellaneous Subjects*

829. Br'er Rabbit

830. Josiah Henson's

831. Thomas Jefferson

832. Rudolph Fisher

833. Frank J. Webb

834.   Jackal

835.   Martin R. Delany

836.   Charles Waddell
          Chestnutt

837.   W. E. B. DuBois

838.   Frances Ellen
          Watkins Harper

839.   *The Autobiography
          of an Ex-Colored
          Man*

840.   *The Souls of Black
          Folk*

841.   *Tropic Death*

842.   Eugene O'Neill

843.   Jake

844.   Sterling Brown

845.   *Quicksand*

846.   Cuba

847.   *Black No More*

848.   Gabriel Prosser

849.   Zora Neale
          Hurston

850.   Archibald J.
          Motley, Jr.

851.   1926

852.   Aaron Douglas

853.   Norway

854.   Malvin Gray
          Johnson

855.   Richmond Barthe

856.   Sargent Johnson

857.   *Bloods--An Oral
          History of the
          Vietnam War by
          Black Veterans*

858.   Lois Mailou Jones

859.   81

860.   *A Raisin in the Sun*

861.   Maya Angelou

862.   13

863.   Nikki Giovanni

864.   Alice Walker

865.   Robert Hayden

866.   Toni Morrison

867.   *The Heart of A
          Woman*

868. Toni Cade Bambara

869. Nikki Giovanni

870. *Spirits in the Street*

871. *The Landlord*

872. *The Cancer Journals*

873. Gayl Jones

874. *The Bluest Eye*

875. Sonia Sanchez

876. ntozake shange

877. Ernest J. Gaines

878. Margaret Walker

879. *The Peacock Poems*

880. *The Living Is Easy*

881. *The Catacombs*

882. Toussaint L'Ouverture

883. Cyrus Colter

884. Malcom Bailey

885. *Divine Comedy*

886. Ralph Ellison

887. *The Autobiography of Miss Jane Pittman*

888. *Sassafrass, Indigo and Cyprus*

889. M. D.

890. Stephen Vincent Benet

891. *All-Night Visitors*

892. *Crisis*

893. Clarence Major

894. Julian Mayfield

895. Bukka Dopeyduke's

896. John A. Williams

897. *The Wig*

898. Al Young

899. *Giovanni's Room*

900. Maud Martha

901. Robert Hayden

902. *Jubilee*

903. Clarence Major

904. Paule Marshall

905. Scipio Moorehead

906. Lorraine Hansberry

907. William Melvin Kelley

908. Meta Warrick Fuller

909. May Howard Jackson

910. Winslow Homer

911. Augusta Savage

912. Works Progress Administration

913. Richard Allen

914. Joshua Johnston

915. Julien Hudson

916. New Orleans

917. William Lloyd Garrison

918. Patrick Henry Reason's

919. David Bustill Bowser

920. William Wells Brown

921. *Uncle Tom's Cabin*

922. California

923. Grafton Tyler Brown

924. *Awakening of Ethiopia*

925. Nelson A. Primus

926. Sargent Johnson

927. Wildfire

928. William A. Harper

929. Laura Wheeler Waring

930. John Henry

931. Ellis Wilson

932. Sargent Claude Johnson

933. Nelson A. Primus

934. William Henry Johnson

935. James Lesesne Wells

936. Beauford Delaney

937. Spiral Group

938. Howard University

939. William E. Artis

940. Selma Burke

941. Gravestones

942. Charles Alston

943. *Magic and Medicine*

944. Norman Lewis

945. Romare Bearden

946. Art Students League

947. Augusta Savage

948. Jacob Lawrence

949. *The Contribution of the Negro to American Democracy*

950. Elizabeth Catlett

951. John Wilson

952. Twentieth-Century Creators

953. Africa

954. Raymond Saunders

955. Lucille Malika Roberts

956. Floyd Coleman

957. God of thunder

958. Mikelle Fletcher

959. Varnette Honeywood

960. Rape

961. Faith Ringgold

962. American Flag

963. Chicago

964. Chicago

965. Barbara Chase-Riboud

966. Karamu House

967. Adelmola Olugebefola

968. John Singleton Copley

969. George Bellows

970. Edward M. Thomas

971.   Karamu House   Sanaa

972.   *Seventeen*   989.   Store-Front
                                           Museum
973.   Walking stick
                                 990.   Cinque Gallery
974.   William A. Harper
                                 991.   The Ile-Ife Museum
975.   *The New Negro*   of Afro-American
                                           Art and Culture
976.   "Art Commentary
        on Lynching"   992.   Art and Soul

977.   Alain Locke   993.   The New Thing Art
                                           and Architecture
978.   1940   Center

979.   Six   994.   "Harlem on My
                                           Mind"
980.   Beauford Delaney
                                 995.   Black Man's Art
981.   Thomas Sills   Gallery

982.   Charles White   996.   "The Evolution of
                                           the Afro-American
983.   Marie Johnson   Artist:1800-1950"

984.   The Anacostia   997.   Boston
        Museum
                                 998.   Detroit
985.   Boston
                                 999.   Mexico
986.   1964
                                 1000.   Knoxville College
987.   "Invisible
        Americans: Black   1001.   *Fred Hampton's
        Artists of the   Door*
        '30's."
                                 1002.   David Hammons
988.   Weusi Nyumba Ya

1003.	Attica Prison	*1021.*	Ben Jones
1004.	Lucille Clifton	*1022.*	Gary A. Rickson
1005.	1970	*1023.*	A nail
1006.	Larry Neal	*1024.*	Three
1007.	Richard Mayhew	*1025.*	Penitentiaries
1008.	Norma Morgan	*1026.*	Seventeen
1009.	Tom Lloyd	*1027.*	*The Raising of Lazarus*
1010.	Marvin Harden		
		1028.	Medusa's head
1011.	20		
		1029.	Pauline Hopkins
1012.	A circle		
		1030.	J. McHenry Jones
1013.	Japanese P.O.W.'s	*1031.*	Boston's South End
1014.	*Why: Black Guernica*	*1032.*	Ohio State Penitentiary
1015.	Harlem Riots		
		1033.	*Caroling Dusk*
1016.	Blue Note		
		1034.	Frank Yerby
1017.	Three		
		1035.	Three
1018.	Raymond Saunders	*1036.*	Melvin B. Tolson
1019.	The Watts Riots	*1037.*	Samuel Allen
1020.	The 1963 church bombings	*1038.*	The 'sixties
		1039.	Mari E. Evans

1040.   W.E.B. Du Bois

1041.   Dudley Randall

1042.   Don L. Lee

1043.   Samuel Ward

1044.   Fenton Johnson

1045.   Washington, D.C.

1046.   Saunders Redding

1047.   *Youngblood*

1048.   Margaret Danner

1049.   *I Am a Black
        Woman*

1050.   Gwendolyn
        Brooks

1051.   Black womens'
        writing

1052.   *South To A Very
        Old Place*

1053.   Addison Gayle

1054.   *Black Fire*

1055.   Audre Lorde

1056.   June Jordan

1057.   Adefunimi

1058.   Jessie Fauset

1059.   Andrea Lee

1060.   *The Soul Brothers
        and Sister Lou*

1061.   *The Chaneysville
        Incident*

1062.   Dr. Martin
        Luther King, Jr.

1063.   *A Soldier's Play*

1064.   Richard Hunt

1065.   Chester Himes

1066.   Liberia

1067.   Boone House

1068.   The abolition of
        slavery

1069.   *The Lynchers*

1070.   *Wedding Band:
        A Love/Hate Story
        in Black and
        White*

1071.   Ed Bullins

1072.   James Allen
        McPherson

1073.   Lucille Clifton

1074.	*Umbra*	*1091.*	*Playboy*
1075.	Robert Hayden	*1092.*	Hal Bennett
1076.	Moses Roper	*1093.*	*Sally Hemings*
1077.	South Sea Islands	*1094.*	*We Can't Breathe*
1078.	Mrs. A.E. Johnson	*1095.*	Leon Forrest
1079.	James Edwin Campbell	*1096.*	*Daddy Was a Number Runner*
1080.	Fenton Johnson	*1097.*	John Edgar Wideman
1081.	Eric Walrond	*1098.*	*Trouble in Mind*
1082.	*Fire*	*1099.*	Black House
1083.	Gordon Parks	*1100.*	*Clara's Ole Man*
1084.	The Vietnam Veterans' Memorial in Washington, D.C.	*1101.*	Dusable Museum
		1102.	Ai (Florence Anthony)
1085.	Alice Walker	*1103.*	James Edwin Campbell
1086.	*Praisesong for the Widow*	*1104.*	Jackie Robinson
1087.	Gloria Naylor	*1105.*	1963
1088.	Ann Petry	*1106.*	Broad jump
1089.	*Runner Mack*	*1107.*	Ferdinand Lewis Alcindor, Jr.
1090.	Cecil Brown		

1108.	Yale University		Union
1109.	Rafer Louis Johnson	*1125.*	Lightweight
1110.	Bill Jones	*1126.*	Skydiving
1111.	Nathan "Sweetwater" Clifton	*1127.*	New York Giants
		1128.	Warren Moon
1112.	David Jones	*1129.*	Roy Campanella
1113.	North Carolina	*1130.*	Broad jump
1114.	Powerboat racing	*1131.*	Kansas City Monarchs
1115.	William "Dolly" King	*1132.*	"Jersey Joe Walcott"
1116.	Walter Payton	*1133.*	Warren Moon
1117.	Valerie Brisco-Hooks	*1134.*	Emmett Ashford
		1135.	Arthur Ashe
1118.	Southwest	*1136.*	Don Barksdale
1119.	William Henry Lewis	*1137.*	The Women's Sports Car Club
1120.	Bonnie Logan	*1138.*	Steeplechase
1121.	Joe Louis	*1139.*	Denver Broncos
1122.	Dan McClellan	*1140.*	"The Magician"
1123.	Webster McDonald	*1141.*	Jack Johnson
1124.	Black Economic	*1142.*	James J.

Braddock

1143. April 10, 1947

1144. Ora Washington

1145. 12 years

1146. Harvard University

1147. William H. Lewis

1148. George Godfrey

1149. Joe Gans

1150. "Homocide Hank"

1151. Howard P. Drew

1152. Edward Gourdin

1153. Eddie Tolan

1154. Jesse Owens

1155. Harold Poage

1156. Livingstone College

1157. The Colored Intercollegiate Athletic Association

1158. 1895

1159. Argyle Hotel

1160. The Cuban Giants

1161. Andrew "Rube" Foster

1162. "Cyclone"

1163. The Big Ten

1164. University of Chicago

1165. Tuskegee Institute

1166. Alfred Holmes

1167. Ora Washington

1168. The International League

1169. 1949

1170. Ezzard Charles

1171. Rocky Marciano

1172. Sydney, Australia

1173. Arthur Ashe

1174. 26 feet

1175. Syracuse University

1176. Marie Thompson

1177.   Inez Patterson

1178.   Joseph Edward
        Trigg

1179.   "Monk" Overton

1180.   Clifton Wharton

1181.   William H. Lewis

1182.   Chock Full o'
        Nuts

1183.   Fenwick H.
        Watkins

1184.   University of
        Vermont

1185.   Boston University

1186.   The
        Interscholastic
        Athletic
        Association of
        Mid-Atlantic
        States

1187.   Rome

1188.   Wilma Rudolph

1189.   Lem Barney

1190.   Dick Barnett

1191.   "Kid"

1192.   Joe Black

1193.   Cornell
        University

1194.   Botswana

1195.   Drag Racing

1196.   Idaho

1197.   Michael Eric
        Carter

1198.   Ernie Davis

1199.   Martial Arts

1200.   Willard Jesse
        Brown

1201.   St. Louis Browns

1202.   The Harlem
        Globetrotters

1203.   Satchell Paige

1204.   Leukemia

1205.   Willie Davis

1206.   Lawrence Eugene
        Dobbs

1207.   Robert Louis
        Douglas

1208.   Kansas City
        Monarchs

1209.	The King-Kennedy Sports and Development Foundation	*1226.*	Mike Garrett
		1227.	Boxing
1210.	Quarterback	*1228.*	Kid Gavilan
1211.	Karate	*1229.*	Althea Gibson
1212.	"Road Runner"	*1230.*	Carlton Chester Gilchrist
1213.	Wayne Embry	*1231.*	Joe Black
1214.	Julius Erving	*1232.*	Montreal Expos
1215.	Richard Evans	*1233.*	Julius Winfield Erving, III
1216.	The Ice Capades	*1234.*	James "Junior" Gilliam
1217.	Rufus Ferguson		
1218.	Middleweight	*1235.*	"Jefferson Street Joe"
1219.	"Tiger"	*1236.*	"Nitro Nellie"
1220.	Wenty Ford	*1237.*	University of California
1221.	National Negro Baseball League		
		1238.	Berry Gordon, Jr.
1222.	Muhammed Ali	*1239.*	Edward O. Gourdin
1223.	University of Michigan	*1240.*	Frank Grant
1224.	"Smokin' Joe"	*1241.*	1974
1225.	Floyd "Jelly" Gardner	*1242.*	Pool

1243.	Robert McCurdy	*1258.*	Jim Parker
1244.	Benwell Townes Harvey	*1259.*	Floyd Patterson
1245.	Marques Haynes	*1260.*	Frederick "Fritz" Pollard
1246.	Dr. Edwin Bancroft Henderson	*1261.*	Frank Robinson
		1262.	Joe Louis
1247.	Silas McGee	*1263.*	Bill Russell
1248.	John B. McLendon	*1264.*	Boston Celtics
		1265.	Bill Richmond
1249.	Sam McVey	*1266.*	Joe Louis
1250.	The National Hockey League	*1267.*	Andrew Foster
1251.	1974	*1268.*	Shinguards
1252.	Ralph Harold Metcalfe, Sr.	*1269.*	Archie Wright
		1270.	Ohio State University
1253.	John Merritt		
1254.	Orestes "Minnie" Minoso	*1271.*	"Giants"
		1272.	Isaac Murphy
1255.	Archibald Louis Wright	*1273.*	61st
1256.	Arnett William Mumford	*1274.*	Marshall W. "Major" Taylor
1257.	Cicero "Brooklyn Kid" Murphy	*1275.*	John B. Taylor
		1276.	"Mother" Seames

1277.	Philadelphia Warriors	*1295.*	Arthur Ashe
1278.	Paul Robeson	*1296.*	Harry Edwards
1279.	Boston University	*1297.*	Harvard University
1280.	1927	*1298.*	Charles Sifford
1281.	Bill Russell	*1299.*	Los Angeles Open
1282.	Harlem Globetrotters	*1300.*	Willie Simms
1283.	1939	*1301.*	Lenward Simpson Jr.
1284.	Satchel Paige	*1302.*	Chicago Cardinals
1285.	Sugar Ray Robinson	*1303.*	Victoria Young Smith
1286.	1948	*1304.*	Hank Aaron
1287.	11 years, 8 months	*1305.*	Sophonia Pierce Stent
1288.	Boston Celtics	*1306.*	George "Never" Sweatt
1289.	Althea Gibson	*1307.*	The Harlem Globetrotters
1290.	Archie Moore		
1291.	Willie Mays	*1308.*	Carlene Hard
1292.	Charles Sifford	*1309.*	"Goose"
1293.	Jim Brown	*1310.*	Marion "Dover" Tolson
1294.	Wilt Chamberlain		

1311. The Hutch Award

1312. Emlen Tunnell

1313. Alton White

1314. Cheryl White

1315. Ruth White

1316. Willie Byron White

1317. The Sullivan Award

1318. Art Williams

1319. 1962

1320. Bill Wright

1321. Louisiana

1322. The Harlem Globetrotters

1323. Gale Sayers

1324. Burl Toler

1325. Mike Garrett

1326. Bill Russell

1327. Satchel Paige

1328. 1964

1329. Muhammed Ali

1330. Charles Liston

1331. Cincinnati Royals

1332. Pete Brown

1333. Wesley Unseld

1334. Mal Whitfield

1335. Edward Temple

1336. Grambling College

1337. Jim Gilliam

1338. 1964

1339. Willie Nauls

1340. Ruth White

1341. Cassius Marcellus Clay

1342. New York Giants

1343. Elston Howard

1344. Archie Clark

1345. Dick Arrington

1346. University of Iowa

1347. Muhammed Ali

1348. Virginia

1349. Frank Robinson

1350. Frank Gilliam

1351. Brooklyn Excelsiors

1352. Aristedes

1353. Fritz Pollard

1354. Akron Indians

1355. 1929

1356. The New England League

1357. Dan Bankhead

1358. 1947

1359. Prairie View Bowl

1360. Roy Campanella

1361. Atlantic Seagulls

1362. Arhur Dumas

1363. John McLendon

1364. Cleveland Pipers

1365. Roberto Clemente

1366. Wilt Chamberlain

1367. Arthur Dorrington

1368. The Harlem Renaissance Five

1369. The "Rens"

1370. Florida A & M

1371. Joe Frazier

1372. Henry Armstrong

1373. Brooklyn Dodgers

1374. Jake Gaither

1375. Eddie McAshan

1376. Leroy "Satchel" Paige

1377. Bud Fowler

1378. John McGraw

1379. The Savoy Big Five

1380. Dave Winfield

1381. Marcus Allen

1382. 1947

1383. The National Industrial Basketball League

1384.   The Masters

1385.   Jim Brown

1386.   Elgin Baylor

1387.   Virginia Squires

1388.   Lee Elder

1389.   Wilt Chamberlain

1390.   Berlin Olympic Stadium

1391.   Bob Gibson

1392.   Theodore Cable

1393.   Althea Gibson

1394.   Reggie Jackson

1395.   Satchel Paige

1396.   Wilma Rudolph

1397.   University of San Francisco

1398.   O. J. Simpson

1399.   The Memphis Southmen

1400.   1924

1401.   National Negro Baseball League

1402.   Minnesota Vikings

1403.   Mobile Bears

1404.   Hank Aaron

1405.   Josh Gibson

1406.   Lou Brock

1407.   "Sweetness"

1408.   Edmonton Eskimos

1409.   James Harris

1410.   Valerie Brisco-Hooks

1411.   Moses Malone

1412.   Charles Sampson

1413.   1975

1414.   Bob Gibson

1415.   His feet

1416.   Ernie Banks

1417.   Compton College

1418.   La Ruth Bostic

1419.   Roy Campanella

1420. George C. Poag

1421. Larry Doby

1422. Mabel Fairbanks

1423. Elston Howard

1424. Isaac Murphy

1425. John "Buck" O'Neill

1426. Willie O'Ree

1427. Jimmy Winkfield

1428. Cleveland Indians

1429. Isaac Murphy

1430. Jim Brown

1431. Cassius Clay

1432. Tommie Smith

1433. George Foreman

1434. John Carlos

1435. Buchanan

1436. Clarence E. "Bighouse" Gaines

1437. Rocky Marciano

1438. 1950

1439. Kenny Washington

1440. Wilbur Jackson

1441. Los Angeles Rams

1442. Rickey Henderson

1443. 1971

1444. Monte Irvin

1445. Daryl Dawkins

1446. Maurice Stokes

1447. The Baker League

1448. 1867

1449. Ohio State

1450. Jackie Robinson

1451. Satchel Paige

1452. Al Downing

1453. Kansas City Monarchs

1454. Frank Robinson

1455. 8 - 0

1456. Kinshasha, Zaire

1457. Cleveland Indians

1458. George Foreman

1459. 1968

1460. A. Molineaux
        Hewlett

1461. Prentice Gault

1462. Jim Jeffries

1463. Frank Thompson

1464. Jess Willard

1465. Fritz Pollard

1466. William
        Craighead

1467. Thurgood
        Marshall

1468. Ernie Banks

1469. Roy Campanella

1470. Curt Flood

1471. Josh Gibson

1472. Reggie Jackson

1473. Don Newcombe

1474. 628

1475. Chicago Romas

1476. Elgin Baylor

1477. Elvin Hayes

1478. Earl Lloyd

1479. "The Big O"

1480. Nine

1481. George Dixon

1482. Battling Nelson

1483. Jersey Joe
        Walcott

1484. Walker Smith

1485. Leon Spinks

1486. Archie Moore

1487. Henry Armstrong

1488. Sandy Saddler

1489. Orange Blossom
        Classic

1490. Tom Molineaux

1491. George Dixon

1492. 110

1493. Beau Jack

1494. Pike Barnes

1495. 14

1496. Willie Simms

1497. The Calumet Wheelmen

1498. Louisville Cubs

1499. Birmingham Black Barons

1500. Charles West

1501. Ernie Davis

1502. Sam Langford

1503. Seven

1504. Dr. Reginald S. Weir

1505. Althea Gibson

1506. Howard P. Drew

1507. George C. Poag

1508. Bingo Dismond

1509. Wilma Rudolph

1510. Tigerbelles

1511. Elvin Hayes

1512. 37

1513. 44

1514. Marshall "Major" Taylor

1515. 1936

1516. Tommie Smith and John Carlos

1517. 1971

1518. Jimmy Winkfield

1519. Huddie Ledbetter

1520. Jelly Roll Morton

1521. Basin Street

1522. Buddy Bolden

1523. Mahalia Jackson

1524. Mamie Smith

1525. Minstrelsy

1526. Jim Crow

1527. Juba (William Henry Lane)

1528. James Bland

1529. *Uncle Tom's Cabin*

1530. Scott Joplin

1531.   Bessie Smith

1532.   Jimmy Yancy

1533.   The Cotton Club

1534.   Teddy Wilson

1535.   Dizzy Gillespie

1536.   James Brown

1537.   Nat "King" Cole

1538.   Miles Davis

1539.   Duke Ellington

1540.   Apollo Theatre

1541.   Ella Fitzgerald

1542.   Quincy Jones

1543.   Sugar Cane Club

1544.   The rent party

1545.   Charles Callender

1546.   Bert Williams & George Walker

1547.   Billy Kersands

1548.   New York City

1549.   *In Dahomey*

1550.   The Lafayette Players

1551.   *Shuffle Along*

1552.   Charleston

1553.   Fats Waller

1554.   The Krigwa Players Little Negro Theatre

1555.   Ridgely Torrence

1556.   Charles Gilpin

1557.   Ethel Waters

1558.   Louis Armstrong

1559.   Eubie Blake

1560.   Billy Eckstine

1561.   Billy Holiday

1562.   Ma Rainey

1563.   Max Roach

1564.   Dinah Washington

1565.   The banjo

1566.   The Coonjine

1567.   Pinker Day (Pentecost

Sunday)

1568. The Bamboula

1569. Congs Square

1570. The Essence

1571. Marvin Gaye

1572. Zip Coon

1573. Edward VII

1574. Sam Lucas

1575. 1915

1576. Bill Robinson

1577. *The Creole Song*

1578. The Cake Walk

1579. *A Trip to Coontown*

1580. Paul Lawrence Dunbar

1581. Bert Williams

1582. Marie Laveau

1583. *Darktown Follies*

1584. Theatre Owner's Booking Association

1585. Florence Mills

1586. Lena Horne

1587. Josephine Baker

1588. Hamsley Winfield

1589. Sammy Davis, Jr.

1590. Hampton University

1591. *Song of the South*

1592. 1937

1593. Asadata Dafora

1594. Katherine Dunham

1595. Pearl Primus

1596. Alvin Ailey

1597. *Show Boat*

1598. Janet Collins

1599. *House of Flowers*

1600. Arthur Mitchell

1601. Geoffrey Holder

1602. 1942

1603. 1902

1604. *The Birth of a Nation*

1605. *The Birth of a Race*

1606. George P. Johnson

1607. Hattie McDaniel

1608. Lorenzo Tucker

1609. Sammy Davis, Jr.

1610. *Black Girl*

1611. Stepin Fetchit

1612. Lou Gosset

1613. James Earl Jones

1614. Clarence Muse

1615. *To Kill A Mockingbird*

1616. *No Way Out*

1617. Richard Roundtree

1618. Isabel Sanford

1619. *The Heart is a Lonely Hunter*

1620. Billy Dee Williams

1621. *For Love of Ivy*

1622. Dizzy Gillespie

1623. Berry Gordy

1624. Ruby Dee

1625. *Affectionately Yours*

1626. Billie Thomas

1627. Pearl Bailey

1628. *Amazing Grace*

1629. Duke Ellington

1630. Farina

1631. *The Autobiography of Miss Jane Pitman*

1632. *Basin Street Revue*

1633. *Benito Cereno*

1634. Cab Calloway

1635. Duke Ellington

1636. Ray Charles

1637. Richard Pryor

1638.	*Carmen Jones*	**1656.**	O.J. Simpson
1639.	Dooley Wilson	**1657.**	Diana Ross
1640.	*Cleopatra Jones*	**1658.**	Otis Young
1641.	*The Comedians*	**1659.**	Ella Fitzgerald
1642.	Niagara	**1660.**	*Lifeboat*
1643.	Amiri Baraka	**1661.**	*The Littlest Rebel*
1644.	Bill Foster	**1662.**	*Lost on the Stars*
1645.	Dr. George Washington Carver	**1663.**	Spearchucker
1646.	Muhammad Ali	**1664.**	*Mahogany*
1647.	Cicely Tyson & Paul Winfield	**1665.**	*A Man Called Adam*
1648.	The "Be Black, Baby" Troupe	**1666.**	Richard Roundtree
1649.	Jim	**1667.**	Mandingo
1650.	*Ice Station Zebra*	**1668.**	*Night of the Living Dead*
1651.	Fredi Washington	**1669.**	Pearl Bailey
1652.	David Ruffin	**1670.**	Vinnette Carroll
1653.	Paul Winfield and Ruby Dee	**1671.**	*Dreamgirls*
1654.	Bill Robinson	**1672.**	*The Wiz*
1655.	*The King and I*	**1673.**	Sidney Poitier & Dorothy

Dandridge

1674. *A Raisin in the Sun*

1675. 1977

1676. Gambia

1677. *Gone With the Wind*

1678. Butterfly McQueen

1679. *The Sailor Takes a Wife*

1680. Scott Joplin

1681. Johnny Mathis

1682. *Blacula*

1683. Isaac Hayes

1684. Richard Pryor

1685. Hattie McDaniel

1686. The Hall-Johnson Choir

1687. Hazel Scott

1688. Redd Foxx

1689. *Sounder*

1690. Sidney Poitier

1691. *Fame*

1692. Sunshine Sammy

1693. Bill Robinson

1694. The Mills Brothers

1695. Robert Guillaume

1696. Sammy Davis, Jr.

1697. Billie Holiday

1698. Michael Jackson

1699. Fats Walker

1700. *To Sir with Love*

1701. *The U.F.O. Incident*

1702. Sam Lucas

1703. Cleavon Little

1704. *Greased Lighting*

1705. *Watermelon Man*

1706. Sherman Helmsley

1707. *Way Down South*

1708. Vicksburg

1709. Wilma Rudolf

1710. Clarence Muse

1711. *The World, the Flesh, and the Devil*

1712. Mango

1713. Tracy Reed

1714. *Young Man With A Horn*

1715. Avon Long

1716. Louis Armstong

1717. Pearl Bailey

1718. Ivan Dixon

1719. Dionne Warwick

1720. *Super Fly TNT*

1721. Sidney Poitier

1722. Aretha Franklin

1723. Esther Rolle

1724. Lawrence-Hilton Jacobs

1725. Gene Anthony Ray

1726. Diahann Carroll

1727. Gladys Knight

1728. Al Freeman, Jr.

1729. Gregory Hines

1730. Garrett Morris

1731. Maya Angelou

1732. *Go, Man, Go*

1733. Etta Moten

1734. Cab Calloway

1735. *Hickey and Boggs*

1736. Louis Armstrong

1737. Louise Beavers

1738. Ray Charles

1739. *King Kong*

1740. Carnegie Hall

1741. Richard Pryor

1742. Diana Ross & Billy Dee Williams

1743. *Let's Do It Again*

1744. *Let the Good Times Roll*

1745. *Live and Let Die*

1746. *Lost Horizon*

1747. "Lift Ev'ry Voice and Sing"

1748. Hugh Robertson

1749. Bill Cosby

1750. Florence

1751. "Ole Man River"

1752. Debbie Allen

1753. Lionel Richie

1754. Mahalia Jackson

1755. A lynching

1756. "Julia"

1757. Diahann Carroll

1758. Shirley Bassey

1759. Berry Gordy

1760. *Lilies of the Field*

1761. Tim Reid

1762. Jimmie Walker

1763. Telma Hopkins

1764. *Jamaica*

1765. Diana Ross & the Supremes

1766. Billie Holiday

1767. Lena Horne

1768. *The Wiz*

1769. Teddy Pendergrass

1770. Clarence Williams

1771. Sarah Vaughan

1772. Ella Fitzgerald

1773. Delegate to the UN

1774. Roland Hayes

1775. Canada Lee

1776. Leontyne Price

1777. Paul Robeson

1778. "Bojangles"

1779. Los Angeles Philharmonic

1780. Ornette Coleman

1781. Max Roach

1782.	Vibraharp		Foster
1783.	Lou Rawls	1801.	Earl "Fatha" Hines
1784.	Coleman Hawkins	1802.	Billy Strayhorn
1785.	Yusef Lateef	1803.	Teddy Wilson
1786.	1923	1804.	Lester Young
1787.	Charlie Parker	1805.	Scat singing
1788.	Eubie Banks	1806.	Paul Robeson
1789.	Teddy Bunn	1807.	Pulitzer Prize
1790.	Alto saxophone	1808.	Willis Richardson
1791.	"Georgia on My Mind"	1809.	Louis Armstong
1792.	The Shah of Iran	1810.	1833
1793.	Dizzy Gillespie	1811.	It was the first successful drama written and performed by blacks.
1794.	Greg Morris		
1795.	Sidney Bechet		
1796.	Canada Lee	1812.	Katherine Dunham
1797.	Willie Smith	1813.	East St. Louis
1798.	James P. Johnson	1814.	Tina Turner
1799.	Huddie "Leadbelly" Ledbetter	1815.	Whitney Houston
1800.	George "Pops"	1816.	B.B. King

1817.   Denise Nichols

1818.   Wynton Marsalis

1819.   Patti LaBelle

1820.   Harry Belafonte

1821.   *Jo Jo Dancer*

1822.   Irene Wilson

1823.   Creativity

1824.   *The Color Purple*

1825.   Oprah Winfrey

1826.   Shug Avery

1827.   None

1828.   Bill Cosby

1829.   Margaret Avery

1830.   Little Richard (Penniman)

1831.   Melvin Van Peebles

1832.   Wilhelmenia Fernandez

1833.   Opera Ebony

1834.   Marian Anderson

1835.   Leontyne Price

1836.   Stevie Wonder

1837.   Donald Byrd

1838.   Stanley Clarke

1839.   Eddie "Lockjaw" Davis

1840.   John Lee Hooker

1841.   J.J. Johnson

1842.   Elvin Jones

1843.   Rahsaan Roland Kirk

1844.   Ramsey Lewis

1845.   McCoy Tyner

1846.   Wayne Shorter

1847.   Gene Ammons

1848.   Mildred Bailey

1849.   1937

1850.   Bobby Timmons

1851.   Art Blakely

1852.   McCoy Tyner

1853.   Lee Morgan

1854.   Max Roach

1874.   Archie Shepp

1855.   Sonny Rollins

1875.   Jimmy Smith

1856.   Horace Silver

1876.   Hot Lips Page

1857.   Stuff Smith

1877.   Oscar Peterson

1858.   Sun Ra

1878.   Bud Powell

1859.   Sonny Terry

1879.   Max Roach

1860.   "Under the Boardwalk"

1880.   Sonny Rollins

1861.   Jive Five

1881.   Pharoah Sanders

1862.   Tamla

1882.   Mongo Santamaria

1863.   Sar Records

1883.   Scott Joplin

1864.   Levi Stubbs

1884.   Yusef Lateef

1865.   16

1885.   "Memphis Slim"

1866.   Jesse Hill

1886.   Ferdinand Joseph La Menthe "Jelly Roll" Morton

1867.   Thelonious Monk

1868.   Four Tops

1887.   Theodore "Fats" Navarro

1869.   Stevie Wonder

1870.   Tyrone Davis

1888.   Ma Rainey

1871.   Wilson Pickett

1889.   Sonny Rollins

1872.   Lee Morgan

1890.   Julian "Cannonball" Adderley

1873.   Horace Silver

1891.	Louis Armstrong	*1910.*	Mary Lou Williams
1892.	Eubie Blake		
		1911.	Lester Young
1893.	Roy Eldridge		
		1912.	Mills Brothers
1894.	Ella Fitzgerald		
		1913.	"It's Too Soon to Know"
1895.	Errol Garner		
1896.	Dizzy Gillespie	*1914.*	"Goodnight Sweetheart, Goodnight"
1897.	Herbie Hancock		
1898.	Jimmy Rushing	*1915.*	"Sincerely"
1899.	Johnny St. Cyr	*1916.*	Flamingos
1900.	Louis Jordan's Tympany Five	*1917.*	Tony Williams
		1918.	Sonny Til
1901.	Bessie Smith		
		1919.	LaVern Baker
1902.	Willie "The Lion" Smith		
		1920.	Orioles
1903.	Billy Strayhorn	*1921.*	Larks
1904.	Big Joe Turner	*1922.*	Rudy West
1905.	Sarah Vaughan	*1923.*	"Pookie" Hudson
1906.	Fats Waller	*1924.*	Moonlighters
1907.	Ethel Waters	*1925.*	"Only You"
1908.	Muddy Waters	*1926.*	1954
1909.	Randy Weston	*1927.*	Tommy Hunt

1928.	Harptones	**1946.**	Allen Toussaint
1929.	Clovers	**1947.**	Big Jay McNeely
1930.	Fred Parris	**1948.**	Ben E. King
1931.	"Deserie"	**1949.**	Leontyne Price
1932.	Johnny Otis Show	**1950.**	George Shirley
1933.	Jimmy Witherspoon	**1951.**	Henry Lewis
1934.	Ruth Brown	**1952.**	William Grant Still
1935.	Junior T-Bone Walker	**1953.**	"Sixty Minute Man"
1936.	"R.M. Blues"	**1954.**	William Grant Still
1937.	Ike Turner's Kings of Rhythm	**1955.**	Leontyne Price
1938.	Bobby Bland	**1956.**	George Shirley
1939.	Fats Domino	**1957.**	Dean Dixon
1940.	Lloyd Price	**1958.**	Leontyne Price
1941.	Guitar Slim	**1959.**	De Paur's Infantry Chorus
1942.	"I Almost Lost My Mind"	**1960.**	Minton's Playhouse
1943.	Percy Mayfield	**1961.**	Miles Davis
1944.	Muddy Waters	**1962.**	Ornette Coleman
1945.	Barbara Lynn		

1963.	Oliver Nelson		
1964.	Newport, RI	**1982.**	Jimmy Charles
1965.	Mary Caldwell Dawson	**1983.**	Coleridge-Taylor Perkinson
1966.	Todd Duncan	**1984.**	Peacock
1967.	Drifters	**1985.**	Dominoes
1968.	"He's So Fine"	**1986.**	Clyde McPhatter
1969.	"I Can't Stop Loving You"	**1987.**	Jackie Wilson
		1988.	Smokey Robinson
1970.	Jesse Belvin	**1989.**	Drifters
1971.	Lou Rawls	**1990.**	"Spanish Harlem"
1972.	Jackie Wilson		
1973.	Roy Hamilton	**1991.**	Shirley Owens
1974.	"Money Honey"	**1992.**	Tamla
1975.	Lowman Pauling	**1993.**	Shep and the Limelites
1976.	Midnighters	**1994.**	Sue Records
1977.	1956	**1995.**	Johnny Otis
1978.	Hank Ballard	**1996.**	Supremes
1979.	Turks	**1997.**	Sylvester Stewart
1980.	Hank Ballard	**1998.**	24
1981.	"Pop Eye"	**1999.**	Jobete

INDEX

"Magician, The", 1140
Mahogany, 1664
Mahoney, Charles H., 688
Mahoney, Mary Eliza, 605
Major, Clarence, 893
Malcolm X, 163, 171
Malone, Moses, 1411
Man Called Adam, A, 1665
Mandingo, 1667
Mango, 1712
Marciano, Rocky, 1171, 1437
Marsalis, Wynton, 1818
Marshall, Paule, 904
Marshall, Thurgood, 182, 1467
Martial Arts, 1199
Maryland, 14
Massachusetts, 12
Massey, Walter (Dr.), 725
Masters, The, 1384
Mathis, Johnny, 1681
Matzelinger, Jan E., 62, 167
Maud Martha, 900
Mayfield, Julian, 419, 894
Mayfield, Percy, 1943
Mayhew, Richard, 1007
Maynard, Robert C., 752
Mayor, 250
Mays, Benjamin (Dr.), 722
Mays, Willie, 1291
McAshan, Eddie, 1375
McClellan, Dan, 1122
McCoy, A.H. (Dr.), 252
McCoy, Elijah, 48, 534
McDaniel, Hattie, 1607, 1685
McDonald, Webster, 1123
McGee, Silas, 1247
McGraw, John, 1378

McHenry, Donald F., 675
McKay, Claude, 232, 418, 805
McKissick, Floyd B., 434, 743
McLendon, John B., 1248, 1363
McNeely, Big Jay, 1947
McPhatter, Clyde, 1986
McPherson, James Allen, 1072
McQueen, Butterfly, 1678
McVey, Sam, 1249
Medusa's head, 1028
Meharry Medical College, 386
"Memphis Slim", 1885
Memphis Southmen, The, 1399
Men of Mark, 669
Meredith, James H., 160
Merrick, John, 20
Merritt, John, 1253
Metcalf Sr., Ralph Harold, 1252
Metropolitan Museum of Art, 314
Mexico, 999
Michigan, University of, 1223
Middleweight, 1218
Midnighters, 1976
Milkman, 818
Miller, Aaron, 798
Miller, Dorie, 595
Mills Brothers, The, 1694, 1912
Mills, Florence, 1585
Milton House Museum, The, 400